VISIONARIES

— ☙ —

VISIONARIES

Bill Mosher

ORBIS BOOKS

Maryknoll, New York 10545

The Catholic Foreign Mission Society of America (Maryknoll) re-cruits and trains people for overseas missionary service. Through Orbis Books, Maryknoll aims to foster the international dialogue that is essential to mission. The books published, however, reflect the opinions of their authors and are not meant to represent the official position of the society.

Published by Orbis Books, Maryknoll, NY 10545-0308

Manufactured in the United States of America

Cataloging-in-Publication Data is available from the Library of Congress, Washington, DC
ISBN 1-57075-024-6

*This book is about the illuminating rays of insight
that sometimes shine on life's path.
In my life, the source of that light has been my wife,
Christine D'Entremont Mosher,
the woman who showed me the way.
And my son,
Matthew William Mosher,
who continues to teach me
the power and beauty
of unconditional
love.*

Contents

The Concept

*We did not want our work
to be judged by the answers
that it provided but rather by
the questions that it inspired.*

THIS BOOK is the true story of the discoveries made by a small group of people who embarked on an extraordinary journey of exploration into the largely uncharted territory of human emotion. We are not scientists connecting people to machines in laboratories or psychiatrists running personality tests on patients in a hospital ward. We are a team of documentary filmmakers who wanted to find the answer to one gnawing question: What is the magic that occurs when one human being helps another?

All of us knew from the outset that even the act of posing the question would seem to some to be superfluous at best and corny at worst. But we wanted to approach the question from a new and different perspective and thought we could present the subject matter in a way that had never appeared on television before.

The idea was simply this. Unlike traditional documentaries, this new television series would not spend its time doing research and collecting data. The program called *Visionaries* was not about facts; it was about feelings.

In every corner of the earth, millions of people make a conscious decision to dedicate their lives to helping other people. If a tiny fraction of the number of people who are involved in philanthropic work made the same kind of decision to perform any other type of activity, there would be entire channels on cable television dedicated to their area of interest. Yet there is not a single television program, nor even regular news coverage, of such philanthropic work, which in the United States alone employs millions of people, controls $800 billion in assets, and represents 7 percent of the Gross National Product.

By way of comparison, consider the entertainment industry, which employs far fewer people and has assets of about $61 billion. There are at least a half dozen programs like *Entertainment Tonight*, an entire cable channel with twenty-four hours of programing, hundreds of radio programs, as well as scores of magazines and newspapers dedicated to the topic. Moreover, the subject matter is covered by every news outlet in the nation as if it were as important as what happens on Capitol Hill.

In the very beginning, it seemed obvious that one of the reasons programs like *Visionaries* were not on the air was because there was a prevailing point of view among television programers that good news does not sell. Therefore, *Visionaries'* second mission was to prove to the world that powerful, emotion-evoking television did not have to be about sex, violence, and human conflict.

With this simple concept, a journey began that would take the crew around the world on the most compelling journalistic adventures we had ever undertaken.

In the beginning, we had no idea where we would go or how we would find the money to fund the project. No television station, cable outlet, or network had expressed an interest in the idea. We had no access to any research on the subject, and no experts in the field lent their support. All that existed was a profound sense of knowing, a gut feeling, that this thing was meant to be.

The proverbial first step in the journey of a thousand miles began with the placement of a few lines of type in a nonprofit trade publication. It announced our desire to produce a thirteen-part series profiling non-profit organizations.

Hundreds of organizations working in every corner of the world called and wrote to express their support. The journey had begun.

This is the story of that incredible two-hundred-thousand-mile odyssey that would take us from a tiny program in North

Carolina to strange and exotic lands where people from every walk of life are quietly involved in simple acts of giving that astonish the mind and stir the soul.

Along the way, we would travel in war zones, consort with revolutionaries, and walk solemnly in the land of the martyrs. The central philosophy of *Visionaries* was to create a sense of shared experience between the individuals being profiled and the viewers at home. Toward that end, we slept in mud huts in Sudan, sailed on canoes down the Orinoco River in the Amazon Basin, and dropped into primitive Filipino villages in a helicopter. In our role as silent witnesses, we saw things no one should ever have to see. We cried often and at least once we almost died, but everywhere we went, another chapter unfolded to reveal startling insights into the very essence of the human spirit.

In the end, the discoveries that we made validated our inner belief that the size and scope of human charity is so all-encompassing that there must be profound forces at work.

But something far more remarkable occurred. After a while, we discovered that each of us, in our own way, was living the story and that we began to practice what was being preached to us.

Ultimately, the television series *Visionaries* succeeded in a way we never could have dreamed because we learned from the lessons that are in this book.

When we first started producing the individual episodes, we said over and over again that we did not want our work to be judged by the answers that it provided but rather by the questions that it inspired people to ask of themselves.

Producing this program has required us to ask these same questions of ourselves. This book provides the answers that have been revealed to us in our own personal quest to discover why we do the things we do. Our answers are not your answers, however. You must come to those in your own way at a time and place that has meaning to you.

Therefore, this book isn't about telling you what to think or what to believe. Its purpose is the same as the television program's. It is about understanding through shared experience.

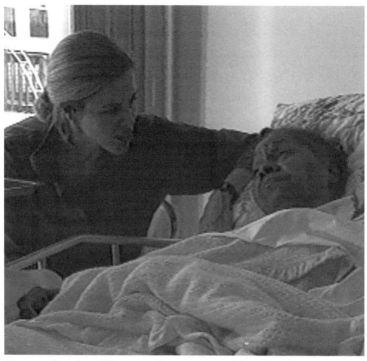
Human Service Alliance volunteers provide a hand, an ear, simple companionship to those who are ill, in pain, or dying.

CHAPTER ONE

The Power of Personal Perspective

*Somehow in their hearts they knew
that something beautiful would
grow in the empty space left behind
when money and ego were removed.*

O N THE WEST COAST of South America, a river, wide and slow, curls around the Ecuadorian city of Guayaquil and oozes its way toward the sea. Along its eastern bank, the incessant din of honking horns pierces the hum made by six million people clawing their way through another day. You clench your teeth shut and inhale tiny sniffs of the thick, pungent air through your nose, taking in the smell of sewerage, rotting fruit, and carbon monoxide in small doses.

On the river bank away from the city, there is some relief. Down a twisting set of wooden steps there is a pier, where a rusty steel-hulled boat, sixty feet long, waits to take on passengers. A narrow gangplank bows in the middle as two figures teeter halfway up. One is a small, barefoot boy inching backward up the plank. The other is an old man, with a scraggly white beard, whose frail body is bent toward the boy. He shuffles forward, seemingly afraid to lift his feet off of the plank.

There is something about the scene that captures your attention and draws you into the moment in a way that makes the scene seem dreamlike. All of your senses sharpen and come into focus. At the same time, the sights, sounds, and smells of the city — that only moments ago seemed all-consuming — fade away.

Just the hint of a smile flickers in the corner of your mouth. It's the same kind of a look that comes over your face when you're listening to someone approaching the punch line in a well-told joke. You don't know what's coming next; you just know it's going to be good.

Then you notice there is a rope knotted around the old man's waist that loops up into the boy's hand. He is using it to lead the man like a dog on a leash. An eerie shiver flickers up your spine.

Thirty, maybe forty people follow the pair on board the ferry that will take them to Durán, a rail-head town on the other side of the river. It's used only by those who can't afford the fifty-sucre (or nine-cent) bus fare.

Not unlike a chapel, simple wooden benches arranged on either side of a narrow center aisle fill the deck. In the stern, protruding up through the floor as if it were an afterthought, is a giant diesel engine. A scrawny, rat-faced man jams the engine into gear. It coughs in protest, and then, reluctantly, the motor pushes the boat away from the dock.

You still have that silly grin on your face, but no one seems to notice. The other passengers all appear absorbed . . . no, the word "absorbed" isn't right. They all seem . . . well, elsewhere. In a way, it is as if you and they occupy a different dimension, each unable to connect with the other. But that realization is liberating in the way it allows you the freedom to observe more intensely in your invisibility.

Sitting right next to you is a frail woman who looks to be in her fifties. She's wearing a dirty, light blue pullover dress hanging loosely from her bony shoulders. Under one arm is a little girl with her bare knees tucked up tightly against her chest as she chews absent-mindedly on the knuckle of her forefinger. The girl shifts a little and snuggles against her mother, who responds with a gentle squeeze of her arm as she crosses one leg over the other. A flimsy leather sandal, held together by a strip of black electrical tape, dangles from her big toe. When the woman turns slightly to look down at her daughter, you see her full face for the first time. She's not fifty after all. In fact, she might be as young as twenty. What you mistook for the wrinkles of age are worry lines that crease away from her sunken eyes and sag from her downturned mouth.

That's when it hits you, and you feel ashamed. What a moment ago seemed to be an honest effort to connect with the poor now feels more like a Third World amusement ride in which the center of attraction is suffering people put here for the rich gringo's perverse entertainment.

Suddenly, there is movement in the front row. The young boy from the gangplank stands and turns at the waist to look back at the skipper manning the engine. They exchange nods and the boy leans toward the old man and whispers something in his ear. Gently, the boy eases him to his feet and helps him sidestep his way out into the center aisle. The man lifts his head and you see for the first time that his eyes have no pupils. A rustling ripples through the crowd. The boy bends over to pick up the rope dangling from the man's waist and walks backward as he tugs gently to guide the man forward. The boy leads him into the space between the first and second bench as the passengers seated there shift their knees to make room. The old man lifts his arms in front of him and turns over his gnarled hands to cup his bony fingers into a bowl. One after the other, each passenger places a coin or a crumpled up bill in the old man's hand.

Dabbles of sunlight reflecting off the river dance through the smoky air and land on the boy's smooth round face as he guides his elder in a wide arc to enter the next row of benches. He cannot be more than seven or eight. You see in his eyes a quiet dignity, and it dawns on you that the old man must be his grandfather, and the boy is proudly serving him in the only way he can. He crosses the center aisle and leads the man toward the woman and child at your side. The mother, who could not afford the nine cent bus fare to Durán, holds a five-sucre note folded neatly in her calloused hand. She's looking straight ahead, seemingly oblivious to the theater being played out in her midst or her role in the drama. In a display of profound understatement, she lets the bill drop from her fingers into the pile as the man mumbles past her.

It's your turn, but you're too stunned to do anything but

fumble with the wad of cash in your lap. Ecuador is a country where a schoolteacher, a nurse, or a civil servant might make only eighty dollars a month. The blind man, his grandson, and their extended family of as many as a dozen people could survive on forty dollars. The money you hold in your hand is enough to feed the entire boatload of people for a month.

What do you do? Do you play the role of the magnanimous gringo and give yourself a cheap high by forking over a crisp twenty dollar bill? But then what have you done to diminish the humble gifts of the other thirty or so people? The stack of sucre notes in the old man's hands looks impressive until you remember that the exchange rate is six hundred sucres to a dollar, and all those five-sucre notes don't add up to thirty-five cents. Not only will your twenty dollars diminish their simple acts of kindness; you cannot know what impact such sudden wealth can have on a boy and his grandfather. After all, it would not be unlike giving a panhandler on the streets of New York a thousand-dollar bill. Would that be wise?

On the opposite end of the spectrum is the option of adding yet another five-sucre note to the pile. However, is that truly an act of charity? Are you really giving anything of yourself? Is there some correlation between the level of sacrifice and the degree of philanthropy? And if so, what's in it for you, the giver?

Days, months, even years later the scene lives on in your mind with a vividness that seems to grow with every recall. At first, it seemed to be a simple but profound statement about the innateness of charity. There on the boat from Guayaquil to Durán were some of the poorest people on earth. You could see how life had beaten them down in their twisted limbs, bent backs, and glazed-over eyes with that distant stare that seemed to border on catatonia. Yet, reduced to its lowest common denominator, the human experience seemed to be about giving. Still, one could not help but wonder what would happen if the same man and boy were to walk down the center of a subway car in downtown New York.

It would seem that the real lesson on the boat to Durán had less to do with charity and was a lot more about the power of personal perspective. Maybe it is only from the twisted materialistic perspective of Americans that comes the idea that serving humanity has anything to do with money in the first place. Because we put such a value on wealth, we suppose that those who don't have it must be deprived. It is in that context of supposed deprivation that we make the leap of logic to assume that if you don't have money you don't have happiness. Even more convoluted is the assumption that if you don't have as much money as I want, then you must be as miserable and unhappy as I would be if I were lowered to your standard of living.

On the surface, these issues might seem esoteric, but when you stop and think about it, the truth is that the question of how people of dramatically different points of perspective serve one another is the fundamental issue of our time.

The artist Robert Henri once said, "People almost never think what they think they think." As a nation, Americans think the issue in Somalia had something to do with greedy warlords fighting over turf and the wealth created by millions of dollars in humanitarian aid. It was really about the world's inept response to the collective desire to help the thousands of people they saw starving to death on the nightly news. The world's prosperous nations responded with charity. Once charity was given, the American psyche was primed, as it always is, for the payoff in a currency called gratitude.

Success was not measured in terms of how many people are alive today who would have otherwise starved to death. Instead, the American public wanted to judge the operation on an applause meter calibrated to measure the degree to which the Somalis appreciated how much we had done for them.

Now, more than ever before, the great debates of our time revolve not around aggression and conflict, but around how one group serves another. In America, when we think we're talking about education, health care, homelessness, crime, drug addiction, and immigration policy, we are really talking about how one group of people helps another group of people. What makes all of this so complicated is the issue of gratitude, or "what's in it for me?" Maybe it is because our society has grown and prospered through a system of barter and exchange that requires the giver to receive something of equal value in return for whatever goods or service the giver provides. Whatever the reason, a stumbling block in mustering support for most social programs is not in demonstrating the delivery of services but in showing that there is a payback for society.

Homelessness is a good example. In the 1980s, there were thousands of people on the streets of America. The media, ever on the hunt for a gut-wrenching story about the downtrodden, milked it for all it was worth until there was a giving frenzy. It resulted in a dramatic increase in the amount of money being spent on the homeless.

At the core of the entire issue was a simple equation. Awareness of suffering added to a sense of empathy equals a desire to give. But the media in its self-appointed role as the caretaker of the public's goodwill grew bored and frustrated by the fact that the problem didn't seem to be going away. In other words, the white knight failed to slay the dragon. You see, another dynamic of all of this is the tendency to see a social problem as an evil and the solution as a good, setting up the necessity of a confrontation in which success is measured in terms of a winner and a loser. This mentality has brought us the war on drugs, the battle against crime, and the fight for welfare reform.

The truth is that today thousands of the people who were once on the street now have a place to live. But the public doesn't see that thousands of lives have been made better. The media in particular and the public in general have difficulty separating the people from the problem. Therefore, when the nightly news does one of its "reality checks," it discovers that there are still as many, if not more, people on the street. It does not seem to matter that thousands of people are receiving services that eventually result in an improved lifestyle for those who truly want help. The "reality" is that society has failed miserably to eradicate a social ill. The re-sult is a phenomenon called donor fatigue. When the average American walks down a city street, he or she becomes per-turbed because there are still people sleeping on the sidewalk. The person lying in the gutter becomes the embodiment of the problem of homelessness. In other words, the person walking down the street sees the person in the gutter and projects his or her frustration revolving around homelessness as an issue on the individual. After giving spare change to faceless people for a year or two and being emotionally engaged in the issue through the media, the tendency is to feel that, Hey, I've been giving for a long time now and I don't feel like the problem is going away. And besides, these people aren't at all grateful for what I and the rest of society have been doing for them. Because society has not been declared the winner and home-lessness forever vanquished, we are chagrined, if not angry, at the people who are suffering through the problem.

It is at this stage that a vicious cycle starts in which ser-vices begin to be withdrawn, ostensibly because the programs are not working. At a deeper, more personal level, the real reason is that the national psyche is extremely irritated and sees the so-called victims as ingrates. More importantly, the body politic acts out its neurotic feelings about the needy in a series of national mood swings that catapult us between dy-namic and innovative social programs to vindictive reforms. The result is we go from drug rehabilitation to mandatory jail sentences for addicts, from building shelters for the homeless to criminalizing vagrancy, and from welfare to workfare.

Why? Because we are not thinking what we think we are thinking. As someone once said, "When a fellow tells me, 'It's not the money, it's the principle of the thing,' it's the money."

Dawn breaks reluctantly over the Piedmont in the upper west-ern part of North Carolina between the cities of High Point, Greensboro, and Winston-Salem. The sun paints soft splashes of burnt orange light across the clapboards of a white farm house sitting atop a gentle rise, overlooking the intersection of Highway 158 and Old Greensboro Road. From the roof peak a songbird glides on outstretched wings to land on a flowering shrub on the lawn that separates the house from the large two-story building thirty yards away.

At sunrise, it is still dark in the hallway that leads away from the reception area down toward the office and the four guest rooms. A single, oblong slice of light falls out of an open doorway near the end of the hall and lands on the shiny brown tiled floor. You step softly forward, reluctant to disturb the stillness you find unexpectedly inviting. In the strange half-light between night and day, there is a sensation of crisp energy in the air. You feel surprisingly alive.

A slight but solid woman comes through the illuminated opening and heads down to the last door on the right. She has short curly hair, serious eyes, and a genuine smile that can light up her whole face. Her name is Susan. She is one of them.

One of them? Yes, one of the two dozen founders of the Human Service Alliance. They came together in 1986. It is hard to explain how or even why. In the beginning, they shared a gnawing emptiness that left them unfulfilled and yearning to discover if there wasn't more to life. There was a physician from Arizona, a carpenter and his family from Alabama, an American college professor who had been teaching in Europe for seventeen years, and a young scientist who came out of the Smoky Mountains to earn his doctorate. Susan is a CPA from Wilmington, North Carolina.

In the last room on the right, a man lies on a bed made up with fresh white sheets. His black, leathery skin hangs loosely from his once powerful frame that now seems to float atop the soft mattress. He lies flat on his back, his arms outstretched at his side with his mouth slightly agape, allowing the air to whistle softly when it leaves his lungs. He senses Susan in the room and lets his head roll to the left. She approaches, leans over him and lays her hand along the side of his face. He smiles ever so slightly in the way a newborn responds to the sight of a familiar face.

His name is Tom Alston. He was once a major league base-
ball player. In fact, he was the first black ball player signed
by the St. Louis Cardinals. Past the foot of his bed, tacked
to the wall are black and white pictures of him in uniform.
In his time and place he was somebody special. He had moments most people only dream about in childhood fantasies.
But that was a long time ago. Now he has only one more thing
to accomplish. Tom Alston must die.

That is not a bad thing. At least not to Susan and the
people who volunteer to take care of Tom and the other guests
twenty-four hours a day from the time they arrive until the
time they die. It all comes back to the power of personal perspective. These volunteers see the world differently. If you ask
her, she'll give you an idea why.

"Working with the terminally ill offers that opportunity to
meet someone and bond with someone for a short time at a
completely different level of experience. It really is soul to soul.
It's one human being loving another human being.

"Here, death is as much a part of life as any other aspect
of life. It's a perfectly natural transition. There may be the
missing of the interaction with that person, but for me, there's
much more joy for having been part of their life, that I was
able to serve them in some way and help make their life a little bit better. And I find it a real celebration of life to be with
people as they make that transition."

Two questions beg to be answered: First, if we can change
our opinion about death, arguably the most dramatic event in
the human experience, what does that say about our ability to
alter our feelings about all matters related to human emotion?
The second question is, How do you do it? How do you take
something like death and turn it into a positive experience?

If you can answer the second question the first answers itself. Susan says, "Every volunteer who comes here brings with
them all of their own thoughts and fears about death and dying. We all bring with us our confidence and lack of confidence
about the ability to take care of somebody who's really sick and
our attachments to what all that means, so by offering that
service, we not only can serve the guest that's here; we all be-

come much more aware of what life is about, what's important about life, what we're able to do that we never thought we could do. We begin to experience the joy that the guest experiences in the smallest things — taking a patient outside to breathe the fresh air and see the flowers. We begin to learn how precious life is. And in that learning, we begin to let go of those issues that we thought were really important."

As Susan sits on the couch in the small office where volunteers gather, the words come out of her mouth like verses in a poem. She has a gentle, soft-spoken way about her that makes you feel that she believes deeply in what she's saying. At the same time, she understands if you can't connect with the feeling behind the words. And it is hard. Because there's a light-year in the three feet separating where you sit and where she sits.

It all comes down to another simple equation. The experience of A minus the experience of B equals the distance between the two. To close the gap that exists between you and the HSA volunteers, you need to understand what life and death has taught them in the last eight years.

In the beginning, there were twenty-four people who had found each other through a bizarre series of coincidences that in retrospect might allow the less cynical to think it may have been ordained. One of the group walked into a convenience store three hundred miles away and saw tacked to a bulletin board a handwritten notice requesting volunteers. One woman was living in Arizona and heard about the organization from a childhood friend who had grown up with her in Hawaii. The carpenter in Alabama caught wind of the group forming and packed up his whole family and moved to North Carolina. Another was a successful schoolteacher from Australia with lifetime tenure who read about the organization and visited the facility on a vacation trip to the United States. She went home, quit her job of twenty-two years, packed her belongings, and returned as a full-time volunteer.

What brought them together was a concept so stunningly simple that saying it aloud only diminishes its power. What the founders of the Human Service Alliance wanted to do was to serve other people in an atmosphere untainted by money or ego. It didn't even matter what kind of service they delivered. It was only important that no one would be charged and no one would be paid in monetary terms or status.

They found an old farm house in Winston-Salem and started out providing respite care for families of children with developmental disabilities. Some of the early group members lived in the farm house and supported themselves in a variety of jobs. Others moved nearby and continued to work in their professions while volunteering up to twenty hours a week. Once a month, there would be a weekend-long board meeting in which they would all come together to focus on the central mission that seemed to run deeper than providing a service. That larger purpose was to explore the magic that occurs when one human being helps another.

They knew early on that the venture was destined to be much more than a social experiment. It was bigger than that because they intentionally upped the ante by investing themselves to a degree seldom seen outside of organized religion or cultism. This was different because they all came from different religious backgrounds and there was no charismatic leader holding the group together.

In the beginning, when no one thought it would last, they persevered by steadily returning to the central theme, that nothing would be charged and no one would be paid. They even refused to bill Medicaid or insurance companies because these groups had not volunteered to contribute.

It was like collective meditation. Those who have never meditated think it has something to do with relaxation and restfulness. Meditation is about thinking about only one thing. By repeating the mantra and gently returning yourself to that single thought whenever your mind drifts, the empty space is created in which spiritual growth can occur.

Something similar happened with the Human Service Alliance. Over and over again, without making it an issue, each volunteer gently returned to the idea that this isn't about me or how am I going to be rewarded for what I'm doing. It's about service. It's about giving.

Slowly, great new concepts took root and grew in the cavernous empty space that was vacated by their egos. Derwin Lackey, a carpenter and a man of inestimable insight, was one of the first to see a simple truth emerging.

"We began to analyze in our brainstorming sessions that when we previously had done things for other people we felt good. We made the connection that we had been motivated by how it made us feel. Everything we had been doing in life had to do with taking in...it all had to do with us. By reversing that flow is where we found the magic. Instead of doing the service because we felt good, we began to do the work because it was a service and because it helped the group. It was out of that group work that the magic appeared."

The idea that you get more out of service when you stop trying to get anything out of it is the first of several great paradoxes that would form the foundation upon which many future ideas would be built. The second is that a higher sense of self-worth can be attained by removing the self from the equation. In the fertile soil created by the steadfast commitment to the idea that no one would ever be paid for his or her service and nothing would ever be charged grew the concept that money was often about ego.

When people started thinking they wanted to be paid, what they were really thinking was, I need proof of my value. Removing the avenue of compensation as a means of reaching personal fulfillment could detour the ego down a more treacherous road: the pursuit of power.

Systems were instituted to remove opportunities for the ego to assert itself. It was decided early on that there would be no leader. All matters of policy would be decided by the full board in monthly, weekend-long meetings. Day-to-day decisions would be handled by a steering committee, the membership of which would be determined by rotating terms.

The ego, however, is a tenacious conniver. If you slam the door on money and power, it will try to find a hole to crawl through. The biggest one was the window to the world created by the need to attract volunteers and financial support. Media coverage would stimulate those resources.

It was the proverbial double-edged sword. Swung one way, it cleared a path to hundreds of people who could serve and be served by the programs and by the concepts growing and maturing in the Human Service Alliance. At the same time, the gleaming edge of public acclaim could easily carve out a big chunk of fame for whoever stood in the spotlight.

Eliminating money from the program is a little bit like quitting smoking. You make a decision. It's final and irrevocable and that's the end of it. Removing the ego is more like dieting, because you can't give up food altogether, just as you can't totally eliminate the ego from the human psyche without dire consequences.

Since complete separation between the program and the world wasn't an option, they decided to install a screen that would allow the air to come in while keeping the bugs out. There would be no designated spokesperson who would assume the public face of the program. Last names and detailed profiles of individuals would be discouraged. More importantly, without anything being said, a persona began to emerge in the group that automatically fell into place whenever a powerful ego came into their midst. Whether the visitors were local politicians anxious to add human service credits to their resumes, public relations wizards or fundraising gurus who wanted to sell them success, or even dynamic volunteers acting out their martyrdom, the group had one response: boredom.

As the years passed, the program grew; and as it did, a new, unexpected truth emerged. When a need arose, resources magically appeared in the form of foundation grants and corporate gifts. A new building was built beside the remodeled farm house. On the first floor, private rooms looking out into the garden would be the last home for people dying of AIDS, cancer, and a multitude of other diseases. Across the hall, rooms were set aside for an herbal therapist, an acupuncturist, and a massage therapist who would work side by side with mainstream physicians to treat people with chronic illness.

The entire top floor was laid out with private rooms reserved for the full-time volunteers who were now arriving from all over the world. They donated from two weeks to six months of their time, working up to sixty hours a week for no pay.

The new reality was that if they didn't do it for the money, they got all they needed. It becomes complicated because you can't see the truth; you can only see its reflection. It's not un-like trying to prove that there is a sun by looking at the moon. You see the moon only because it's illuminated by the light from the sun. At night, you would not know there was either without the reality of both.

It had something to do with immersing yourself in the day-to-day activity and releasing yourself from the outcome.

In the beginning, most members of the group had little or no money. Many had uprooted themselves, leaving behind jobs and other resources. Others were changing careers and others were still in college working toward advanced degrees. Partly out of necessity and partly through an innate sense of knowing, they all consciously released themselves from the de-sire to acquire personal wealth. It wasn't because they thought money was bad. It was because they believed that if they got up every day and committed themselves to service, the rest would take care of itself.

You can never prove such an idea is true just as you can never absolutely prove there is a sun by only looking at the moon. But the reflection is so strong that the truth is hard to deny.

Todd, a successful research scientist whose father is a former attorney general of North Carolina, speaks from experience. "I remember living in the old farm house when we had no heat and we took turns getting up in the morning and starting the wood stove to get the place warm enough for the rest of the volunteers to get out of bed. Most of us had nothing. Today, I think it is fair to say that every single member of the original group is better off both professionally and financially."

Eight years after the first board meeting, almost every member of the original group is still involved. In all those years, no one has ever missed a single weekend-long monthly board meeting. Of the original twenty-four people, eighteen were single. Now they have all married, most finding partners within the original group. There has not been a single divorce or separation.

All those who wanted to be employed now have good jobs and are in most cases earning more money and have more material wealth then they ever had before. Todd was a struggling grad student who is now a scientist doing research at the nearby university. Another was a hosiery salesman who became a program director at a local community college. Another member of the board went from being a college professor to the director of a program for juvenile delinquents. The volunteers are doing so well, in fact, that in 1993, they contributed $40,000 of their own money to the cause.

Eight miles from the Human Service Alliance complex is a new neighborhood called Mystic Glen. There on Discovery Lane, single-family homes are being built by a contractor who is also a member of the HSA board. He and his wife, a full-time volunteer, are selling the homes to other members of the board for below-market prices.

It is mid-morning now and the room at the far end of the hall is warmed by streams of sunshine flickering through the trees, creating gnarling shadows that dance across the sheets covering the man in the bed. Amber particles, suspended in the air, give form to the light. Inside one beam, the dust sparkles as the breath from the man's mouth causes it to swirl.

In the dark corner created by the partially closed curtain, you stand with your hands folded across your waist. You are staring straight ahead, transfixed by the churning dust. Over your right shoulder are the pictures of the ball player in his youth, long before the cancer began to spread out from his colon and devour his life.

The time has come to let go. You don't know how you know, you just do. So you stand and wait. There's nothing left

to do. After all, it never had anything to do with doing anyway. Doing things was just a cover for being. When you came
in during the middle of the night and emptied the bag connected to his body by a tube, it was only an excuse. Sure, it
needed to be done. But that's not why you did it. You did it
because it was a way to be with him, to share his space and be
in his world, just the two of you.

After a while, you both began to understand the act of service for what it really was. It played the same role in your lives
as language. When you speak to another person, it's not the
act of talking that is important. Often it doesn't even matter
what is being said. What matters is that you are communi-
cating, that you are connecting in a time and place that you
share, that you are being, together.

Now, suddenly, there is nothing but you and him. All of your
awareness is focused on the churning particles of dust. You are
so alert, so very alive, you can see, hear, feel, and taste the very
fabric of life in the room. Then it happens. It's as if you see it
through a magnifying glass. One by one the molecules of float-
ing dust ease out of their disorder and become totally still. You
see his lips, still moist . . . his eyes still reflecting light . . . but
you feel the all-powerful sense of emptiness, and you know
he's gone.

It's the ultimate paradox of life, that at the moment of maxi-
mum human disconnection you experience the true depth of
how tightly we are one. It is from this vantage point that power
of personal perspective is truly realized. Standing at the bedside of a person who no longer exists allows you to see the
world differently. What you discover is that the secret is in the
nothingness.

Somehow in their hearts they knew that something beautiful would grow in the empty space left behind when money

and ego were removed. They knew it would happen because they believed in the nothingness. They had felt it before and were blown away by its awesome power. At the bedside, they saw what few had seen before. They saw that the nothingness isn't nothing after all. It's love.

CHAPTER TWO

Caution:
Sixteen Thousand
Children Ahead

*What really matters is what happens
in that magical instant when a little
boy sees love in the eyes of a woman
who has come from the other
side of the world to be with him.*

O N THE HORN of Africa, near Kenya's border with
Sudan, a great upcropping of black rock juts unexpectedly out of the flat earth. Nearby, a little girl
squats beneath a solitary tree, its gnarled limbs twisting defi-
antly above the barren plain. She wears only a tattered white
shirt. Her pointy elbows are propped atop her knees and her
round chin is resting in the crux of her palms pressed together.
Her wide, round eyes are transfixed on a distant dot beyond
the thatched roof huts that is growing ever larger against the
cloudless sky.

It's a vintage DC-3 cargo plane, the word UNICEF embla-
zoned across its side. The aft cabin is filled with a strange
assortment of cargo. There's an old beat-up copy machine,
thirty dozen eggs, and a used Raleigh bicycle. In the front, behind the pilot and co-pilot who are visible through an open
passageway, a dozen seats have been temporarily latched to
the floor. In the second to last seat, a fifty-six-year-old woman
from Wichita, Kansas, is looking out the window, a broad smile
stretched across her face. She is motioning toward the ground
and mouthing a word toward the two men sitting behind her.
You can't hear what she's saying over the roar of the twin en-

Judy Mayotte, refugees advocate, arrives in a war zone.

Southern Sudan, rebel checkpoint.

gines and the whistle of wind blowing through cracks in the fuselage. Finally she yells, "It's Lokichokio." You nod politely in acknowledgment, but remain bewildered at the exuberance that lights up her face. The woman's name is Judy Mayotte, and the experience you are about to share with her will change both of your lives forever.

Loki, as it is called by those who have been there, is an aberration — a weird oasis in a vast expanse of human suffering that stretches a thousand kilometers west and north through the whole of southern Sudan. The camp began in 1989 with a few pup tents and a half dozen relief workers camped out near a makeshift runway. It was meant to be a launching pad for shipments of food and supplies that were being flown into war-torn Sudan. It has become much more. Loki may just be a portal through which we can see the full potential of international humanitarianism.

Sudan has been at war with itself for three of the last four decades. In the north, a Muslim fundamentalist government had been fighting to put down a rebellion started by the Sudanese People's Liberation Army that has at various times controlled large portions of the south. More recently, however, the rebels have been fighting among themselves, having split along tribal lines.

The interfactional fighting and the ongoing war with the north have forced huge segments of the 6 million people who lived in southern Sudan to flee from one battle after another. Over 1.3 million have been killed and another 2 million have been displaced by the war. The survivors are disconnected from their source of food, and hundreds of thousands of people teeter on the edge of survival.

Often the level of malnutrition will reach 80 percent among children, and with malaria, diarrhea, and acute respiratory infections, more children die in Sudan before the age of five than almost anywhere else on the planet earth. That's the bad news. The good news is something you will never see on the nightly news.

— ⊛ —

The fat wheels of the plane shriek as they hit the packed gravel runway. Whizzing by the window, you can see clusters of people huddled outside huts of woven straw. They look like malleable clay figurines baking under the blistering sun.

The plane twists around at the end of the runway and takes up a position beside a row of massive tan tents the size of ware-houses. They are filled with burlap sacks of sorghum, piled in cross-hatched stacks eighteen feet high. Sitting back on its haunches like a proud reptile, the DC-3 points its nose toward the sky. The double doors creak open, and a set of stairs drops to the tarmac. Stepping to the doorway you're smacked in the face by a wall of brutally hot air. You are jolted back, but then you shake it off and wade into it. The thickness of the air is so palatable you actually reach out with your arms and push against it to balance yourself as you awkwardly make your way down the steps.

The small group of passengers slowly shuffles toward a sliver of shade beneath one of the wings and waits as a shiny new mini-bus crosses the runway just before a giant Hercules cargo plane thunders down the runway, throwing up a cloud of dust.

Judy Mayotte is the first one on the bus for the short ride to the camp. She's nodding happily at everyone she sees. She apparently doesn't feel the heat. You've known the woman for a total of nineteen hours and already her sense of exuberance is having an impact on you. It's getting on your nerves. You're beginning to wonder if producing a television series profiling the work of non-profit organizations was such a good idea after all.

Someone said, "Creativity is like throwing mud against a wall; some sticks. Some doesn't." *Visionaries* was just that, an idea that stuck. There was no grand scheme, no great master plan. In fact, the very essence of the concept was that there could be no plan, no script, not even an outline of what the first set of shows would be about.

In the beginning, there were only two assumptions and one

guiding principle. The first assumption was that television is awful. The folks at Human Service Alliance might say it is because television is the altar at which America worships money and ego.

The second assumption was that, because of the failing of television in particular and the media in general, we have a twisted perception of the world we live in. The nightly news, tabloid TV, and so-called reality programing, such as *America's Most Wanted* and *Cops*, bombard us with images that would lead the most optimistic individual to believe that our lives are comprised primarily of horrible nightmares. It goes back to personal perspective. If we see the world from the vantage point of television, our perception can only be that life is a fundamentally unpleasant experience interrupted by occasional triumphs pulled off by people who all look like movie stars.

The most important thing to realize is that the second assumption simply ain't so. The overwhelming preponderance of objective evidence proves beyond the slightest doubt that the world is spilling over with remarkable acts of human kindness and that human beings and the lives they lead are on balance good.

The problem, of course, is that in the eyes of the media, stories about goodness don't sell newspapers or draw viewers to the tube. The sad fact is that they are right. The question is, Why?

Social scientists have done a lot of yammering over the years trying to answer this question. In the process, they have demonstrated a stunning grasp of the obvious. We didn't need a Gallup poll to know that we are titillated by sex, enthralled by violence, and mesmerized by the failings of our idols. The question isn't, Why does playing to our lowest emotions sell? We all know the answer to that question intuitively. The real question is why good news doesn't.

The problem may be that television has not yet stumbled across the right formula. Every decade or so, a new genre comes to the airwaves and brings with it a whole new way of looking at the world. Situation comedy teaches us to laugh at ourselves. Talk shows introduce millions of viewers to people and subjects they would never confront in their daily lives. Documentaries take complicated facts and make them understandable, thereby expanding our minds. Dramas in the "movie of the week" format make it possible for millions of people to connect with contemporary issues like spousal abuse, adoption, infertility, date rape, and sexual harassment by viewing the subjects from an emotional outlook.

So far, no one has stumbled across a method of exploring the part of the human condition that drives a huge segment of the world population to forsake money and fame to pursue the as yet undefined rewards of philanthropic work.

In a country in which entire television channels exist with round-the-clock programing to explore the wonders of cooking, skiing, and travel, there is not a single half-hour of national programing about what may be the most important subject on earth.

Part of the problem is that television consistently uses approaches that continue to fuel the belief that there is no market for the subject. The first is the nightly news puff piece. This is usually the last story of the broadcast. You'll know this one is coming when Peter Jennings smiles, cocks his head condescendingly, and says, "Now, just so you won't think the world is all bad, we have this story from the Children's Hospital in . . . " click.

The puff piece isn't really about understanding the reasons why people give of themselves. It's about playing with our emotions and conjuring up a dose of sympathy. Why? Because news outlets and the people who work in them genuinely want to make a contribution to the greater good. They are as sick of the bad news as the rest of us and in their gut want to believe that their role is helping rather than hurting. The puff piece is about making them feel good and at the same time answering the growing howl from critics of television who want to see less violence and negativity. They accomplish this goal by doing what television does best. It elevates a personality to the pedestal of sainthood.

The second method television uses to address issues related to the world of philanthropic work is the flies-on-the-face approach. These stories are put together by the reporters that relief workers in places like Sudan call famine tourists. They come in with their Banana Republic flack jackets and laptop computers to concoct a documentary or news segment using a potent mixture of horror and pity. The result is that the victims, no matter whether they are mothers in refugee camps in Rwanda or children in a cancer ward in Boston, are so dehumanized and robbed of dignity that the public can't move beyond feeling sorry for them and develop a true human connection with the victims or the people who are serving them.

The last treatment is the documentary approach. This is the dispassionate examination of topics like war, hunger, homelessness, and crime on the streets. Usually, the ominous voice of a narrator guides us through the subject matter, slowly building a case through interviews with one talking head after another. The hope is that through the accumulation of data we will develop a cognitive connection with the people affected by whatever issue is being presented, and through this intellectual understanding of a given topic, we will be moved to action.

Ironically, a hint at what might be the cornerstone of a new approach to bringing good news to television is presented by the programs that have demonstrated just how low we will sink in the pursuit of ratings. "Reality" programs like *Rescue 911* initially drew large audiences because they relied primarily on true stories of people in crisis. Through the interweaving of documentary style interviews with re-creations of real events, the viewers developed a sense of shared experience. The problem, of course, is that the experience being shared was most often fear. Nonetheless, the public became aware of many unheralded acts of heroism, and in the process we learned about subjects like CPR, fire prevention, and child safety that could ultimately save hundreds of lives.

Maybe, just maybe, the answer to the challenge of exploring what happens when one human being helps another could be in the concept of shared experience. What if the viewer could be a silent witness in the lives of ordinary people who were committing extraordinary acts of human kindness? What if you removed the ominous narrator, the flak-jacket-clad reporter, and the corny re-creations and just allowed the viewer to share the experience of, say, working with the more than twenty million refugees and the additional twenty-six million who are internally displaced from war, civil strife, and persecution?

If you were going to do such a thing, you would be a silent witness to the life of a woman like Judy Mayotte.

It's early evening. The sun has drifted below the horizon, but lingering rays of warm light beam from behind the earth's curvature, casting a pink dusting on the fluffy underbelly of the dark clouds overhead. In the center of the camp is a knoll of trees that surrounds a large green canvas mess tent. Narrow dirt paths lined with painted stones snake away from the hub toward the thatched-roof *tukals* spread out over three acres. They house the staff of UNICEF, the World Food Program, and twenty-five different private charities that work together out of Loki in a joint effort called Operation Lifeline Sudan.

You sit quietly at the end of one of the long tables set up outside the mess tent. Ovals of yellow light dance down from the multicolored lanterns strung between the trees around the dining area. You watch as a cacophony of workers arrives down the winding paths. They wander in twos and threes out of the dark shadows that now envelop the scene, the way a campfire creates a bubble of light in the dark forest.

You are struck by the faces. It's as if you are in a gallery of living portraits from every corner of the earth and every facial image has a story to tell. Somehow you feel that if you study them closely enough you will learn all that they know, see all that they have seen, and maybe even acquire the modest self-assurance that comes only to those who have been to the precipice and back again.

A short, compact doctor with a shaved head stands in the food line scooping up a ladle full of hearty stew. There is a perpetual smile pushing up into his pale cheeks, but a weighty sadness tugs at the corners of his eyes. He's talking with a woman whose wide brimmed Stetson sits on the back of her head. Her dark almond-colored face beams through rosy cheeks and her narrow, exotic eyes seem to hint at secrets she is dying to reveal. He is from the midwestern part of the United States; she is from Eritrea.

The dozen tables fill with workers fresh off the planes that carry them in and out of the war zone of southern Sudan every day. Agricultural experts from Sweden break bread with health professionals from the Islamic African Relief Agency sitting at the same table with volunteers from Australia, France, Yugoslavia, Holland, England, Ireland, Belgium, and Norway.

It's an ever-changing mural of the world, an exotic weigh station where bonds are forged in the time it takes to pass the salt or butter your bread. You feel like the world has come home for Thanksgiving dinner.

It's dark now; the air has cooled. As people finish their meals they wander from table to table, telling stories, exchanging messages, and gossiping. You hear names of places like Nasir, Pochala, Bor, and Akobo bandied about. They are some of the twenty-three locations where Operation Lifeline Sudan delivers the food and supplies that feed 1.5 million people a day.

Judy Mayotte is perched on the edge of her chair listening intently to a young couple who are field workers for the World Food Program. Judy's legs are crossed in front of her and a small notebook rests on one knee. She nods in agreement and jots down a few lines. The woman's name is Julie. Her soft blond hair is falling loosely out of a pony tail. She is unadornedly beautiful. Her partner's name is Ed. His foot is propped up on a chair, and he's looking down at Judy. He takes off his beat-up safari hat and sets it on his knee. He pushes his fingers through a mop of curly brown hair and then gestures with an upturned hand as if to say, "I don't know, what do you think?" Judy nods and writes a few words without looking down. The conversation eases to a conclusion and the young couple — she's from England, he's from Seattle — wander off to the hut they share. There is no hint that their lives will intersect again. No foreshadowing.

You're watching her through the crowd. Judy's lips purse together and curl inward as she slowly scans the scene. She pulls in a long, slow breath through her nose. Her eyes close and her head tilts back ever so slightly. In that instant, insight flashes. You suddenly understand one of the things that make her tick. Judy Mayotte has come home. She's inhaling the scent of Africa, drinking in the nectar of camaraderie with people who are changing the world.

Her head lowers again and a smile beams across her face as if to punctuate the declaratory sentence her gesture has spoken.

Now it's your turn to shake your head, because with every insight the mystery deepens. How can a woman, born and raised on the prairie of Kansas, feel such a bond with Africa?

She was born in Wichita, the third of four children. Her father was a successful CPA and a prominent local businessman. She doesn't talk about him much, but it is clear that there was a problem between father and daughter.

When Judy was thirteen, her father determined that she wasn't working hard enough. To instill a sense of discipline, he removed her from the family and sent her off to a Catholic boarding school in Colorado. It did not matter that he had great animosity toward Catholics. What was important was that they were good disciplinarians.

At the boarding school, Judy found something that had been missing in her life. First of all, it was safe. She no longer had to live in an atmosphere of fear caused by her father's drinking. Maybe more important, she was free to be a child, to live in an environment that nurtured her love of life and provided her with strong, competent women as role models. Though her mother had dedicated her life to her children, her role in the household was overshadowed by the overwhelming dominance of her father. Among the nuns, Judy grew and blossomed. It was sometime during this period that she decided to become a Catholic and a nun herself.

Once her father got wind of the fact that Judy wanted to become a Catholic, he took her out of the boarding school and enrolled her back into the public school system. Her world was shattered, her safe haven gone.

It's strange how traumatic memories, like raw nerve endings protruding from our consciousness, have the potential of being charged with either positive or negative energy. Judy's childhood experience could have crushed the spirit in another. Instead, it seemed to have created sensitized connecting points in her personality that allowed her to develop a special empathy for children and families torn from their homes.

In 1991, word spread throughout the relief community that a remarkable event was taking place just south of Ethiopia on one of the great dusty plains of Sudan. The story really began years earlier when a unique consequence of the war caused thousands of young boys to be separated from their homes and families. When a boy reaches the age of nine or ten, it is the custom in many parts of Sudan for him to assume the responsibility of caring for the small herds of goats and other livestock that are among the primary sources of food for each village. This job requires them to lead the flock away from the village in pursuit of fresh grasses.

The relief community, in many instances, anticipated the need to evacuate certain areas and helped move the families to safe havens west and south of the battle zones toward the border with Uganda. But because the boys were away from the villages, they could not take advantage of the truck convoys that moved the villagers to safety. All sides in the war used slash and burn techniques that destroyed their villages and slaughtered their herds, driving them further and further from their homes As this scenario occurred over and over again throughout southern Sudan, many of the boys were forced to flee to the east into Ethiopia, where they gathered together in refugee camps.

In 1991 a coup occurred in Ethiopia, and a new government took over that was unsympathetic to the thousands of refugees hiding on its border. The children were forced out.

The event that stunned everyone occurred when as many as seventeen thousand kids, mostly boys, banned together in one massive force and began an incredible march back through Sudan with the hope of reaching Kenya. They had no food or water, and a thousand kilometers of barren plain separated them from safety. But boys who would be carrying Star Trek lunch boxes to the bus stop if they happened to have been born on another continent stepped forward. They banded together, cared for each other, and formed a massive extended family. The names and deeds of those who took the lead are already forgotten by the world, but because they possessed the raw courage to lead others into the unknown, thousands followed them into the war zone. When the government of Sudan learned that thousands of their own youth were trying to make their way across the eastern tip of the country, they responded with a genocidal plan of attack. They ordered planes into the air that dropped antipersonnel bombs on the children. The seventeen thousand hungry children presented a threat because they were organized and had spent time in a refugee camp supported by the rebels in southern Sudan.

Every morning when the group uncurled and assembled again, the ground was littered with those who didn't make it through the night. Some died of wounds they had received the previous day. Others starved to death or died of diarrhea or other diseases, and still others were carried off into the night by the hyenas and lions that followed the group like circling vultures. Hundreds, maybe even thousands, were buried along the way by the young children in solemn rituals played out day after day.

— ❧ —

A white jeep leaves a churning cloud of red clay dust in its wake as it pulls away from the small runway in Kakuma, located eighty miles south of Kenya's border with Sudan. Judy Mayotte is sitting sideways in the front seat dividing her attention between the back seat and the scene through the front window. Sally Burnhiem, an information officer from UNICEF who is assigned to work with Operation Lifeline Sudan, is sitting behind the driver. Sally points to a black and white sign posted alongside the road:

CAUTION

16,000

CHILDREN

AHEAD

Kakuma is where the vast majority of survivors of the great trek through Sudan now live, along with another fifteen to twenty thousand refugees of the war. Judy Mayotte is here as a representative of Refugees International, a Washington-based advocacy organization. The essence of her mission is to share the experience of those who have been driven out of their homes by the war. Only then can she fulfill her larger role as a spokesperson for those who have no voice. Her journey to the Kakuma camp may not have been as dangerous as it was for the children, now visible outside the windows of her jeep, but her road has been long and it has been arduous. And the hardest part is yet to come.

In the back seat, Sally Burnhiem is explaining how the children first arrived in Lokichokio in June of 1992. There was not an adequate supply of water, and because of the camp's proximity to the border, the children were vulnerable to attack from the Sudanese military. The international community quickly rallied, and Kakuma camp was built deeper inside Kenya. Wells were drilled and latrines laid out in advance of their arrival. A collection of private charities moved in to provide health care and emergency food supplies. Food-for-work programs were established for the able-bodied children to encourage them to build their own houses, using indigenous materials and traditional methods of construction. Unlike many refugee camps, there were no canvas tents or huts constructed out of brightly colored plastic tarps.

Working under the umbrella of the UNHCR (United Nations High Commission for Refugees), more private groups or NGOs (non-governmental agencies) arrived to set up educational programs for the ten thousand school-aged children. Other NGOs began work on trying to reunite the children with their families and treat the emotional trauma they experienced on the road to Kakuma.

Sally leans forward and taps the driver on the shoulder, pointing up ahead to a stand of trees along the banks of a dried-up river. There is a splash of freckles across her pleasant round face, and she speaks with an accent of her native Australia. The jeep pulls off the dirt road and comes to a stop outside a high fence that encloses an open-air church built beneath the shady trees. Judy and Sally step out of the jeep into a melodic wave of singing voices that echoes up from within the walls and cascades back down from the treetops. The rhythm of the African chant is uplifting in a hypnotic way that makes you feel like you have stepped into a slow-moving dream. There is an opening in the fence-like wall and a gauntlet of welcoming faces guides you toward the doorway. As you pass through the entrance, you are enveloped in a sea of singing children. They are standing in a seemingly endless line of irregular rows bellowing forth with upturned heads and lips puckered into perfect circles.

Judy moves into the crowd. Heads turn toward the woman with the short gray hair and dangling earrings. She looks like she wants to stop and hug everyone she sees. When she makes eye contact, the boys seem to blush at the affection they sense in her smile; then they turn quickly back to their song. Like a flash of intuition it becomes awesomely vivid. The colors are brighter. The scent of the air is sweeter, and the music is remarkably beautiful. During that precious instant, you know absolutely, positively, without question, that you are living inside the fragile bubble of awareness that floats between objective reality and spiritual certainty. That is where the magic is made, right there in the space between Judy's smile and the little boy's blush.

The lesson you learned back at the Human Service Alliance in North Carolina takes on new meaning. It isn't the service that is important — that is only a vehicle. What counts is that you make the connection. Yes, Judy has come to Africa, yet again, to share the refugee experience with the world's homeless. And yes, she will take what she has learned back to the United States and, through Refugees International, try to rally the developed world to respond to their needs. She will write newspaper articles for the op-ed pages, appear before congressional committees, give speeches to community groups, talk to students in schools all across the country — and it will all have an impact. But what really matters is what happens in that magical instant when a little boy sees love in the eyes of a woman who has come from the other side of the world to be with him.

Judy steps to the front of the crowd and the song eases to a close. She is introduced and the boys applaud. She talks about how important it is for them to get an education and tells them about the time she was a schoolteacher.

Teaching school was a chapter — a definitive portion of her life story — that had a beginning, a middle, and a conclusion. It was the start of an emerging pattern in which whole careers and ways of life would blossom, bear fruit, and then pass away. The road toward teaching began on the last day Judy saw her father alive. It was the day she was baptized a Catholic. Because of her father's opposition, she was forced to wait until her eighteenth birthday to convert. She was home in Wichita on semester break from college. Her father was at his accounting office when he learned about what she had done. He sent word for her not to come see him because he did not know if he could control his anger. She went to see him anyway.

There was no question that he loved his family, but sometimes he seemed rigid and dismissive of ideas that conflicted with his own belief — yet there was always a hint of softness in his eyes. It was as if he wished he could let down his guard and feel the emotions that his daughter spoke of when she explained what drew her to the church.

He had spent a lifetime building a facade around his soul and now he wore it like body armor. He turned his back to her and looked out his office window, surveying the city's commercial district from his lofty perch. It was his world, his life. Neat structures of concrete and steel. Every building, every office, every storefront and cubicle established the parameters of an individual's life. Walls...that was what it was all about: living within clearly defined boundaries. Whatever confinement the walls created was a small price to pay for the demons they kept inside.

Now his daughter, his own flesh and blood, had scaled the wall. Worse still, she was traversing an uncrossable border into a world he did not understand.

She talked, he listened, but the sound of her words was defeated by the roar of emotion screaming to escape. For the first time he let some of it out. He talked about his belief in a God, about there being something out there beyond his comprehension. When he talked, his back was turned, but his voice was soft and he looked out the window beyond the buildings into the sky. It was there that father and daughter connected. After a while, having said all he could, he turned to leave her in the empty office. As he passed toward the door he reached out and laid his hand on her shoulder. She felt it linger there, years of suppressed affection pouring through his fingers. It meant everything. A month later he was dead. To this day she still feels the touch.

About the same time, Judy contracted polio. She battled the disease, teaching herself to walk all over again while continuing her quest to become a nun. Without parental permission and delayed by her illness, she couldn't enter the convent until she was twenty-one years old. Then her dream was realized. In places like Chicago, Phoenix, Milwaukee, and Kansas City, she was able to stand in front of a classroom of students filled with the same emotions she had experienced as a young girl and return the gift given to her by the nuns in the Catholic boarding school in Colorado.

— ✥ —

It's hard to tell the story now. The journal you kept faithfully throughout the trip ends abruptly on the flight to Ayod. Try as you might, you've never been able to fill the empty pages. It's not reliving the pain, the horror, the fear that stops you. It's something else. Something much less comprehensible.

Maybe if you just let it go. Do it now. With the cold green light of your computer monitor glowing through the dark, sit back and watch the words flow onto the screen.

The images come like flashes from a slide projector, chit-chinging into your consciousness. There's Judy climbing off the plane onto the grass clearing alongside the dirt runway. She walks into the crowd of naked children surrounding the plane. Julie and Ed, the two monitors from the World Food Program, are there also, lingering in the heat, their eyes blinking to adjust to the bright sun. Sally Burnhiem, our Australian guide, is talking to a boy with a gun slung over his shoulder. It's a big ugly M-something-or-other with a fat clip of shells jammed up into the magazine. What catches your eye is the trigger. It's shiny. Most of the metal on the weapon is the color of tarnished steel, except for the trigger. A finger has squeezed against it so often it's polished.

Although the boy wears no uniform, you know he is a soldier in the Nasir rebel faction headed by Riak Machar, who split with John Garang's ragtag army of revolutionaries a few years earlier. Garang, the recognized leader of the rebellion, holds a doctorate from Iowa State University. Both forces have been fighting in and around Ayod for years. It's a place washed in blood and scarred by famine.

The group begins to move. Paul Van Ness, the camera-man, lifts the one-piece Sony Betacam to his shoulder. A child trots up beside Sally Burnhiem, who is leading the way. He reaches up and takes hold of her hand. Together they walk, like mother and son, toward a group of men at the end of the runway. Standing among the soldiers is a tall, regal-looking man dressed in the long white formal shirt Muslims wear to receive guests. He's leaning on both hands set atop a crooked cane stuck in the ground. All around him weapons are laid out in neat rows on the ground or stacked in tepees so they can be snatched up at a moment's notice. The men under his command are working nearby with machetes, clearing clumps of grass from the runway.

Sally and Judy approach him respectfully. His name is Elijah, and he is the commander of the rebel forces in the region. He smiles and gracefully extends his hand in welcome. They ask if it would be all right for the group to go to the edge of town and witness the airdrop of emergency food scheduled to arrive. He nods and offers to lead an armed escort to the drop site.

Single file, the group trudges up a hill along a path worn through the tall yellow grass. A soldier jogs ahead with a tripod mounted machine gun bouncing on his shoulder. Elijah pauses at the edge of a large clearing a hundred yards wide and two hundred yards long. He delivers a frank assessment of the military and political situation in good English as the video crew and the two food monitors figure out how to shoot the airdrop.

A vantage point is selected on the opposite side of the field to avoid shooting directly into the sun as the plane approaches. The group steps into the field. Someone stumbles. There is a sudden gasp. They look down to see what the person tripped over. It's a human skull. The field is filled with the skeletal remains of hundreds of men, women, and children. They are just a few of the three hundred thousand people who starved to death in southern Sudan in recent years as all sides in the conflict continue to use the denial of food as a brutal weapon of war. Starving to death carries a stigma so powerful that the dead are moved outside of town in disgrace and abandoned without burial. It's on the forbidden field of bones that the food to keep the rest of the village alive is dropped.

On the opposite side of the field, the grass is shoulder high. Julie leads the group to a small clearing of matted down grass as her partner struggles to communicate with the Ilyushin aircraft piloted by Russian mercenaries. He's talking in radio lexicon saying things like "Whisky Oscar," and "Do you read me?" He lifts the walkie-talkie to his ear trying to decipher the crackling sound as the slow moving craft passes overhead. He nods to himself as he listens and then lowers his radio and calls out that the pilot wants the group to move further away from the drop site.

Forty or fifty yards further away, Julie and Ed take up positions in front of the camera. They begin to explain that the aircraft, which is visible on the horizon, has completed a wide circle and will fly directly over the drop site to release thirty-one tons of food packed in hundred-kilo sacks. Julie looks into the camera, points toward the plane growing ever larger, and says, "What will happen is that the plane will make two passes, dropping sixteen tons on each pass. The bags will come out on pallets, but they will separate and rain down individually."

"Whisky Oscar, Whisky Oscar, you're cleared to drop," Ed yells into his walkie-talkie. You see the plane lumbering back and forth between Ed and Julie and suddenly you remember the horror stories that came out of northern Iraq. That was when the United States tried to stop thousands of Kurds from starving to death by airlifting food into their mountain sanctuary. The result was that the starving refugees rushed toward the descending food and were crushed to death.

But wasn't that a much different situation? You wonder out loud as the plane seems to be coming from the wrong direction to be flying parallel with the drop site. Julie looks over her shoulder at the plane. There is a quizzical look on her face, but she nods and points out that the only real danger is if the plane were to drop either short or long. That's because they have laid out two giant targets at either end of the long field. All the pilot has to do is connect the dots and he's over the drop zone.

You're not aware of anything going on around you. You see only the plane hovering ever closer. It seems to be flying perpendicular to the drop site and heading directly for you. It's huge and the sound of its jet engines fill the air like a freight train roaring through a mountain pass. A giant prop-driven Hercules aircraft usually delivers the food out of Lokichokio, but this shipment is coming out of Khartoum, the capital of enemy territory in the north. It's part of a United Nations negotiated settlement in which the fundamentalist government has agreed to redistribute recently harvested crops in exchange for seeds and other relief supplies. The people in the village shudder at the sound of the jet engines arriving from the north because they sound just like the bombers that killed so many over the years.

Julie turns back over her shoulder at the plane. Her eyebrows are furrowed and she looks over at Ed and says, "It does look as if it's well over this way, doesn't it?"

A few seconds pass as she locks in on the plane again, and her mind references what she sees with all the other food drops she has monitored in the past. She turns back and looks you straight in the eye. She's calm . . . cool.

"I think we better move over this way." Urgency builds in the span of the single sentence and everyone is in full flight before the words are out of her mouth. Paul drops his camera to his side and runs. It's still rolling.

Julie is running with her head turned toward the sky. "Ed," she pleads. "Ed, tell 'em to stop. Ed, tell 'em to abort."

"Abort, Whisky Oscar. Whisky Oscar, abort. Do you read me? Abort," Ed gasps into his walkie-talkie as he leaps through the tall grass, looking frantically into the sky.

Julie looks up and sees it's too late. The pallets are coming out of the plane. "Fuckin' aye," she screams bitterly.

The grass is gnarled around your feet. You can't get up speed. You look up and the sky is filled with layer after layer of onrushing bags. You stop, plant your feet and take them head-on, knowing this is the place you're going to die. A hundred yards away the first bags are already hitting the ground like a wave of machine gun fire headed your way. You lock onto a single bag plummeting toward your head. Behind it you see hundreds more, like an endless battalion of space invaders on a video game, but it's that one bag tumbling head over heels that's got your number. It's all you can handle. Just that one bag. You bob to the right, twisting your shoulders and your feet follow. The bag hits with a sickening thud and tumbles away. At the same instant, a hundred more spray all around you.

There's a faint, woeful scream mixed in with the sound of the bags splattering across the landscape. You can't get enough air into your lungs. Emotion is coming on in waves like a sudden illness. There's a sense of relief, but the fear refuses to subside. You wonder if it's because of the scream as you try to talk yourself back to normal. You stumble toward the voices hidden in the grass. Someone gasps and someone else lets out a guttural moan. Then you hear Judy's voice. "I'm hurt," she says. "It's my leg. It's really bad. The bones are sticking out all over."

You crash forward, stumbling headlong toward her voice. Then you see her. She's on the ground, her head is cradled in Paul's arms. His camera is resting at his side. You circle around, not knowing what to do, not knowing if you can handle what you're about to see. Then it hits you. Julie's words scream inside your skull. "They'll make two passes, dropping sixteen tons on each pass." My God, they're coming back again. You look to the sky and the plane is circling for another run.

There's hysteria. Ed is screaming in his walkie-talkie. "We have injuries, do you read me? We have injuries. Do not, I repeat, do not drop again." A garbled Russian voice responds. Ed screams louder, the plane completes its circle and settles in for another approach.

Sally is in the middle of the drop zone running through the field of skeletons toward the village. By a stroke of fate, her roommate, an OLS physician, is in the village conducting a medical assessment.

You're on your knees now. Waves of dizziness and nausea are washing over you. Judy calls your name. You can see the blood flowing out around the bone that is protruding out of her calf. The plane is still closing in. "Don't let this stop the show," she says weakly. "Please."

The blinding light from the sun is forcing your eyes into a squint and you're soaked from head to toe in sweat. You kneel at Judy's side, take her hand, and whisper assurances you don't believe. Paul is still holding her and they begin to pray together. Nearby, Ed is passing through the grass, seething into the walkie-talkie. The plane is on its final approach. Then, out of the corner of your eye, something in the grass gets your attention. It's the flashing red light on the camera that is still rolling. You crawl forward, pick it up, and rest it on your knee. Through the viewfinder, you see Paul Van Ness pouring dribbles of water onto Judy's parched lips.

You've never operated a television camera in your life and you have no idea why you are doing it now. Maybe it's an escape. A convenient shield to hide behind...a filter through which to view what you must look at, but can't bear to see.

While you're looking through the lens, Ed lets out a sigh of relief. You look up and the walkie-talkie falls from his mouth to his side. Over his shoulder, you can see the plane breaking suddenly out of its approach and circling away toward the north.

The doctor arrives along with three nurses from an Irish NGO called CONCERN. They work frantically to stop the bleeding and ease the excruciating pain. Bandages are applied and injections of morphine are pumped into Judy. A canvas stretcher is placed beside her and she lets out a scream as she is lifted onto it. Men from the village hoist Judy onto their shoulders and slowly the march back across the field begins. Not a single bag is anywhere near the drop site.

CHAPTER THREE

A Life to Lead

> *The magic is that millions*
> *of people, at least for a brief*
> *period, are transformed into*
> *caring and loving individuals*
> *because of what they know.*

WITH GUNS still slung from their shoulders, the soldiers of the SPLA carried Judy from the field like a fallen warrior. Under the oppressive midday sun it seemed, then as now, like a solemn rite of passage. While in many ways the worst was yet to come, there hung in the air the awesome realization that life could never be the same again. Another chapter in Judy Mayotte's life had come to a close.

Maybe the idea of chapters isn't a good analogy. It's more like she is a recurring character in a series of novellas. There is Judy Mayotte, the child of the prairie: a fun-loving kid who manages somehow to find excitement and joy under the thumb of a domineering father who dislikes Catholics. Next, there is Judy Mayotte, the nun. In that story, a young woman is baptized a Catholic at the age of eighteen. She waits patiently for her twenty-first birthday so she can legally join the convent. A full decade goes by as she travels around the country living a quiet but fulfilling life as a sister and teacher. Then an event occurred in Rome. It was called Vatican II. The Catholic Church, in a bold and dramatic document, fashioned a new view of religious life. Hundreds of nuns and priests reassessed their roles and many, including Judy, returned to secular life.

With fifty-six dollars in her pocket, she headed home. Judy Mayotte took a job teaching juvenile delinquents locked up in reform schools so she could earn the money to return

to college to earn a doctorate. At the height of the anti-
war movement in 1968, she arrived at Marquette University,
where, for some, free love and psychedelic drugs were as much
a part of the college experience as term papers and basket-
ball games. Because she was older and needed a way to pay
her way through school, she took a job as the supervisor of a
women's dormitory. From this vantage point, she became involved in the issues of the day and worked with black women
students and peace activists. Together they struggled to come
to grips with prejudice and war and to find their place in a
world swirling with change.

A new story opened one day in 1972 on the campus of Marquette. Her doctoral course work had been completed, and
she was working on her thesis in the college dormitory. A message arrived that there was someone downstairs who wanted
to see her. It was a man she had met years earlier when she
had taken a summer job doing office work in a local plant
for a large multinational company called Square D Electrical.
She hadn't seen him since his promotion to international vice-
president, after which he transferred to Chicago. His name
was Jack Mayotte.

His life was in crisis. A divorce was looming. There were
six children, four of whom had special needs. The strain had
destroyed the marriage. They talked. A month later he called
her on the telephone. They had dinner. Three months later
they are married.

Looking back on that period, Judy always refers to it as the
happiest time of her life. It was like living in a cocoon of joy in
which the most elusive commodity in her life, unconditional
love, surrounded her. A happier, more confident woman grew
in Jack Mayotte's arms, and in that place they shared she began to fold back the layers of hurt and see what was inside.
She learned to love herself.

Then suddenly it was over. Cancer swept Jack Mayotte
away after only three years. In just a few agonizing weeks between diagnosis and death, it all slipped through her fingers
and she was alone again.

In the following years, Judy accepted every change with

grace. That did not mean that there were not inner turmoil, deep torment, and many painful moments along the
way. What it meant was that she seemed to have a knack for
understanding what circumstances were beyond her control
and making what adjustments were needed to find happiness within the confines of her new situation. After Jack's
death, she went to work for the WTBS television station in
Chicago and became a producer on the Peabody and Emmy
Award–winning series *Portrait of America* hosted by Hal Hol-
brook. Later still, she became an associate and acting director
with the William Benton Fellowship in Broadcast Journalism,
a University of Chicago program for mid-career journalists.

Since Jack's death, there had been a lingering emptiness
that was easy to attribute to losing the man she loved. As
time passed, however, Judy began to realize that there was
something else going on inside of her and slowly she began
to shape a vision of life that was entirely different from anything else she had ever done before. At various times she
would try to put a label on the nebulous urging inside of
her. It was a calling, a desire to serve, a need to play a role
in the world, an inner knowing that it was what she was
supposed to do.

The motivation was indefinable, but the image that kept re-
appearing in her mind was the pictures of refugees she had
seen on the nightly news. One day, out of the clear blue, she
simply decided that she needed to go overseas and work with
people who had been driven from their homes by violence.

She joined the Maryknoll order of nuns with the hope of
going to Africa, but her heart condition made it impossible
for her to serve in a foreign country. Another reality, another
adjustment. She approached her desire from another angle.
She applied for a grant to write a book about the plight of
refugees, and the MacArthur Foundation came through with
the money.

At the age of fifty-one she began a whole new life. She
traveled around the world alone, living in refugee camps in
Cambodia, Pakistan, Eritrea, and Sudan. Dr. Mayotte, child
of the prairie, former nun, widow, and Emmy Award–winning

television producer, talked her way into war zones, hitched rides on cargo planes, slept in mud huts, showered with a bucket and ladle because of an inner belief that you only understand — truly know — what you live.

In the process of writing her book, *Disposable People?: The Plight of Refugees*, she connected with an international network of people who had dedicated their lives to helping the twenty million refugees of the world and the thirty million people who have become internally displaced within their own countries. In the process, she discovered the power and need of something called advocacy. She was invited onto the board of the Women's Commission for Refugee Women and Children and eventually became the chairperson. She joined the board of the International Rescue Committee, and she became friends with Sue Morton, the founder of Refugees International.

Refugees International is a small, Washington-based advocacy organization that, despite its tiny budget, is a loud and articulate voice for the millions of people who continue to be victimized by war. Judy became a member of the board and an active volunteer who traveled the world addressing the ever-fluid needs of the refugee population. Judy Mayotte became one of the world's leading advocates.

Advocacy is a two-pronged scepter used to pierce the consciousness of the world. The first prong represents the issue. There are advocates for virtually every cause from gay rights and prayer in the schools to democracy in Myanmar. The second component of advocacy is global awareness.

It all comes back, once again, to the idea of personal perspective. If you accept the presumption that our view of the world plays an active role in determining who we are, you have opened the door to the possibility of fundamental change through awareness. You can become another person through the simple and natural process of knowing.

When the public *knows* other human beings are suffering, thousands of individuals *become* concerned and caring people.

thousands of individuals *become* concerned and caring people. Democratic governments respond because elected representatives *know* the people who elected them support that action. That's how social advocacy works.

It all seems so simple. Create an atmosphere in which people can learn about something, and change will occur. What often happens, however, is that we get so caught up in the power of creating change that we don't see the real miracle. It's like a magician on stage. We see him putting a rabbit into a hat. He swings a wand, mutters a few words, and, puff, a dove flies out of the hat. We're so mesmerized by the sight of the dove we forget that it's all a trick. The magic isn't that a rabbit was turned into a dove. That never even happened. The magic is our altered sense of reality.

When millions of people become aware of human suffering, the magic isn't the dove that flies out of the public consciousness to save the suffering people. The magic is the altered sense of awareness. The magic is that millions of people, at least for a brief period, are transformed into caring and loving individuals because of what they know.

This is an enormously difficult concept to accept. The usual response is, "Hey, what do you mean millions of dollars in humanitarian aid isn't what's important? Think of all the people who are alive today because people answered the call to action."

The sad fact is that the call to action was necessary in the beginning because of a fundamental breakdown in awareness. Almost all famine is the result of war. War is always between people who are convinced of the differences rather than the sameness of other human beings. That reality, the belief that other human beings can be fundamentally different, is the state of being in which the essential ingredients of conflict breed. When ignorance cohabitates with fear, the offspring is inevitably violence.

Refugees International and the thousands of advocacy organizations around the world play a powerful role in eliminating the ignorance and easing the fear. As they stab away at us with information about the plight of refugees, the rights of mi-

norities, or the dangers of drunk driving, we are consistently
pierced by the realization of our sameness.

Villagers lined the pathway from the drop site to the grassy
air strip and watched solemnly as the white American woman
was carried on the shoulders of young black men who had
been born and brought up in Ayod. Elijah led the march. His
head was bowed and his walking stick was stuck up under one
arm. There was still an unmistakable quiver in the hands that
hung heavily at his side. The seasoned soldier, who had been
fighting a bloody war for all of his adult life, had looked up
at falling bags and saw the face of death. He was headed into
seclusion. It would take three full days, during which time he
refused to see or talk with anyone, to come to grips with what
he had seen.

Most of the seats had been removed from the cabin of the
plane to make way for Judy's stretcher. As she was eased up
toward the open door, she let out a scream. Her lower leg had
been broken in twelve places, the femur collapsed, and the hip
bone was protruding through the skin, causing excruciating
pain every time it moved.

It was dark inside the cabin of the plane. There was a
dazed and distant look on Sally Burnhiem's face as she took
up a position near the head of the stretcher. She brushed
back Judy's hair and absorbed her pain as if it were her own.
Dr. Bernadette Kumar, a native of India, knelt at the foot of
the stretcher and held on to the wooden frame in a white-
knuckled grip as the plane began to accelerate down the grass
strip. Two nurses who were both scheduled to finish their tour
of duty and return home to Ireland the next day took up positions on either side of the stretcher. As the engine revved,
they lowered their heads and gritted their teeth, steeling themselves up for the rough trip down the runway. Paul Van Ness
was strapped into a seat looking straight ahead with vacant
eyes. The quiet and introspective cameraman's open heart had

been profoundly wounded by what he had been through. It would be his last *Visionaries* shoot.

You take hold of the stretcher with one hand and give Judy the other so she will have something to squeeze when the pain comes. The fuselage is vibrating, the engine is whining, and the group circled around Judy have their eyes clamped shut knowing what she is about to feel. The scream comes like hot knitting needles being slowly pushed ever deeper into your ears. Cold sweat drips down your back, tears fill your eyes, and the white bulging fingers sticking out of her vice-like grip pulsate in pain. You concentrate on the ache and in a twisted bit of logic, it feels good.

The plane lifts off into the air and suddenly it's over. Judy releases her grip and sucks in two quick breaths of air and then seems to drift off. In the cockpit the two pilots are talking coolly into their mouthpieces coordinating a plan with OLS personnel two and a half hours away in Loki. It's at that point you realize that Loki is only the halfway point. You're in the heart of the largest country in Africa, and the nearest hospital is a whole nation away in Nairobi, Kenya.

The pilots are Bob Gustin and John Beiter, who work for a non-profit organization called Air Serv. Air Serv's pilots are a rare breed of men and women who leave behind the comfort and security of jobs in the United States and Canada to volunteer to fly relief missions in war zones and areas of famine. Every time their plane hits an air pocket they hear Judy's screams louder than anyone.

The pilots need to make a choice. If they level off at a high altitude the air will be more stable. But in the unpressurized cabin, the higher the altitudes, the more Judy's leg will bleed. They talk over the situation with Dr. Kumar, who crawls up to the cockpit and kneels between the two pilots. She turns around and looks back at Judy. Beneath her stretcher, drops of blood are seeping through the canvas and forming a pool on the floor of the plane. They opt for the lower altitude.

The doctor and the nurses struggle to keep pressure on the wound to minimize the bleeding without causing more pain. They have pain medication in their medical kits, but must

use it sparingly because of Judy's heart condition and because
it can inhibit clotting and cause vomiting, particularly in a
moving plane.

The members of the medical team, struggling under incredible stress, feel the impact of the oppressive heat inside the
swaying plane and take turns using the air sickness bags.

Back in Loki, camp manager Ognjem Predja, a Yugosla-
vian national who has served UNICEF in Nicaragua, Angola,
and Bosnia, is efficiently organizing an emergency action plan.
Word goes out over walkie-talkies and two-way radios. It res-
onates with the kind of clarity an "officer in trouble" call
receives when broadcast over a police radio in a big city. The
reaction is instantaneous and unequivocal. One of their own
is down.

A crew rushes to the airport and tears open a tool shed
beside the runway and quickly begins to construct a tempo-
rary operating room. In distant villages all over Sudan, medical
professionals drop what they are doing and jump into planes so
they can be on the ground in Loki when Judy arrives.

A giant Hercules cargo plane is about to drop a load of sorghum on a village deep in Sudan when it receives the word. It
changes course and heads back to Loki. It's the fastest plane
in the fleet and can take an hour off the final leg from Loki to
Nairobi.

Every need, every detail, is anticipated. The hospital in Nairobi is notified. Her blood type is announced over the radio
and throughout the OLS network. A dozen donors come forward and are transported to Nairobi so the blood will be there
when she needs it. Someone even goes to Judy's room at the
base camp, packs up her bags, and hand carries them to the
airport at Loki so she will have her belongings with her on the
trip to the hospital.

It's a logistical miracle. But then again, OLS is something of a
miracle in itself.

In 1988, over a quarter of a million people died in southern Sudan from the war and a devastating drought. In other words, in one year, five times as many people died in southern Sudan as all of the Americans killed in Vietnam throughout the entire conflict. To respond to the crisis a unique approach was established by the international community. UNICEF and the World Food Program, two mammoth United Nations relief organizations, formed a partnership of sorts. UNICEF would assume responsibility for coordinating relief efforts and providing supplementary feedings for children and other groups in immediate need. In addition, UNICEF would institute programs to bolster the people's ability to care for themselves by providing seeds for planting and tools for harvesting. They also created programs for health care, immunization, and education.

The World Food Program took on the enormous task of delivering as much as 250 metric tons of food from the base camp in Lokichokio and Khartoum in the north to sites throughout all of southern Sudan. At the same time, they built into the delivery of food the concept of food-for-work programs. Through this method, roads, bridges, and schools were built by a labor force paid in food.

The partnership of these two organizations was called Operation Lifeline Sudan. This cooperative effort was not in itself unique. What makes OLS different, and more successful than any other project of its kind, are two powerful concepts. The first was the idea that OLS would be an umbrella that would protect anyone who wanted to help. This philosophy of inclusion transformed what is often an atmosphere of competition into one of cooperation. Private charities from all over the world responded. They came into Lokichokio with a mission. It could be the delivery of emergency medical aid or a desire to rebuild the education system. OLS, rather than seeing that as a threat to its turf, viewed it as a new resource, another tool. To allow the tool to do its job, OLS responded by giving the private charity support in areas like transportation, security, and coordinating their work with others.

The second concept that ultimately made it all possible was called transparency. This meant that OLS would have no secrets. Everything it did would be open and visible to all sides in the conflict. Because OLS has been so extraordinarily successful, it is easy to lose sight of the fact that there is a war being fought. The United Nations is routinely invited into situations like Sudan by the sovereign government. In this case however the government in the north was fighting against its own people, and all sides in the conflict were using the interruption of the food supply as a strategic weapon of war.

In the beginning, a tripartite agreement between the United Nations, the government of Sudan in the north, and the Sudanese People's Liberation Army was hammered out. This document allowed relief workers unrestricted access to the civilian population regardless of which side controlled the area. In the ensuing years, an unwavering commitment to neutrality has run into many obstacles, and relief workers have been harassed and killed. But the leadership of OLS keeps returning to the table, keeping up a dialogue with all sides.

You're standing outside the emergency room of Nairobi Hospital in Nairobi, Kenya. Six hours and a thousand kilometers separate you from Ayod and the nightmarish field littered with bleached white bones. Judy is inside being prepared for surgery. A sensation of emotional relief begins to mix with the physical exhaustion. Judy is not going to die.

It's hard to stand, so you lower yourself into a squat and then finally just sit on the ground with your back against the outside wall of the hospital. The sun is low in the sky, and flickers of light flash through the trees. Hazy, slow-moving images play against the blur created because you're too tired to focus your eyes.

You see Judy being rushed into the makeshift operating room inside a tool shed on the runway at Loki. A nervous crowd hovers about, watching through the open door as she is finally anesthetized and her leg immobilized. The monstrous Herc, engines whining, taxis toward the scene. Then you see again the most absurd of images replayed in your mind's eye.

The belly of the Herc is filled with pallets loaded with bags of
sorghum. Judy has to be carried over them to reach the part
of the cabin where she can be strapped to the floor for the
two-hour flight from Loki to Nairobi.

A sound jolts you back to the here and now. You stand up
and out of the corner of your eye see a station wagon racing up
the embankment that leads from the street to the emergency
room door. It screeches to a stop right in front of you. A white
woman jumps out from behind the wheel and bolts past you
through the open door.

You're dazed. You sense an urgency but are too numb to
respond so you stumble away. Vaguely, you notice that the
hatchback door of the car is open as you shuffle past. There's a
groan. You turn. Sticking out of the back of the car, five bloody
bodies are stacked, head to toe, one on top of the other, like
cordwood.

The woman rushes back out of the emergency room door
leading two pairs of orderlies carrying stretchers. One of them
crawls into the back of the car and grabs hold of the body on
top and turns it over. The man's forehead is crushed and his
eyes are open and vacant. The hospital attendant rolls him out
of the way and gropes for one of the heads below. It's a woman.
He sees something in her eyes and crawls backward out of the
car. Taking hold of her legs he drags her free of the gnarled up
bodies and with the help of his companion they place her on
the stretcher and rush her inside. Signs of life are found in two
more and they too are brought into the emergency room.

The driver of the car stands beside you, gnawing on the
knuckle of her thumb. Finally she turns and looks at you, then
back at the two dead bodies in the back of her car and speaks
with a British accent.

"There was a car accident. I just happened by. No ambulances in this bloody city." She pauses and then motions
toward the car. One of the bodies is that of a black woman
dressed in a neat, tan pinstriped suit. Her limp head dangles
grotesquely over the edge of the tailgate.

"Those two. They went through the windshield," she says
and then draws a long, slow breath that lifts her sagging shoul-

ders. She turns and looks up into your eyes and whispers, "God, almighty, what do I do with them?"

— ☙ —

A man in cerulean blue hospital scrubs crosses by the glass wall inside the Intensive Care Unit at the Mayo Clinic in Minnesota. Judy Mayotte sees him coming. She's conscious and alert.

She remembers everything. Running through the high grass in her long skirt. Her right leg, weakened from the polio she contracted as a teenager, twists and she stumbles to the ground. She turns and looks up; horror contorts her face. The sky is filled with tumbling projectiles angling toward her. There's a sickening thud.

She remembers Paul holding her...the awful heat. And she remembers lying there as Ed yells into the walkie-talkie, "Abort, do you read me? Don't, I repeat, don't drop..." and she calls out, "No, don't stop the drop. I'm all right. The people need the food."

There was a hazy period after the seven hours of surgery in Nairobi. She drifted in and out of sleep, but whenever she was awake, no matter what time of day or night, she saw a familiar face beside her bed looking up into her eyes. Maryknoll nuns and others from the relief community stayed by her side in shifts twenty-four hours a day.

After five days, she regained enough strength to chance an emergency evacuation back to the States. She was taken from Nairobi Hospital, accompanied by a doctor and a nurse, and placed on board a Swiss Air flight bound for Zurich. The rear two seats of the plane were folded down and her stretcher was fitted in against the window. An oxygen mask hung overhead. The doctor and nurse sat beside her and took turns holding her hand. They constantly monitored her condition, concerned about her heart and her reaction to the myriad drugs they had administered to control the pain and stave off infection. A curtain was installed to separate her from the rest of the passengers, but Judy asked that it be kept open.

In Zurich, she recalls being carried through the cargo door and lowered to the tarmac on a scissor lift. An ambulance waited nearby to take her to a hospital to spend the night until her connecting flight the following day.

A storm was hammering the Chicago area as the Swiss Air flight approached late the following day. An ambulance plane from the Mayo Clinic had been dispatched to meet her at O'Hare International Airport, but the small plane could not land in the storm and was diverted to Midway Airport.

At O'Hare she remembers her niece Kathy and Dr. Mary Annel, a Maryknoll sister and practicing physician, coming down the aisle of the empty plane. They were allowed onto the plane to sit with her while an immigration official came on board to process her entry into the country. Her passport had been lost during the accident, but a letter from the American embassy in Nairobi was accepted in its place.

Then came another ambulance ride, this time with sirens blaring and lights flashing. They plowed through rush hour traffic to Midway Airport, where the ambulance plane waited.

But it still wasn't over. As the small craft approached Rochester, Minnesota, the weather threatened to force the pilot to another airport that would put Judy several hours away from the hospital. The doctor did not know if Judy, severely weakened by the long trip, could survive another long, bumpy ambulance ride through a storm. The pilot decided to chance an instrument landing at Rochester.

Now, after ten days in the Intensive Care Unit, the respirator has been removed. Surely, the worst is over. But why is the doctor, clipboard in hand, looking so solemn? He is beyond the glass partition weaving his way toward her. A nurse intercepts him. A smile flashes across his face. If she could only hear what they are saying. Out of the corner of his eye, the doctor looks toward her as he listens to the nurse. Judy and he make eye contact. The smile melts from his face and she sees his shoulders sag ever so slightly.

He breaks away from the nurse and walks backward to finish the conversation on the move. Then he turns fully toward Judy and walks through the door deliberately.

The leg, he explains, is shattered, crushed by the force of the blow she received. It's possible, barely so, but possible, that after a year or two of reconstructive surgery it could be saved.

There is a long pause. Judy's eyes fill with tears. She bites softly into her lower lip and nods for him to continue. The other option is she could have the leg removed now — amputate it below the knee and get on with her life.

The child of the prairie, former nun, widow, Ph.D., Emmy Award winner, author, and advocate says, "Take it off. I've got a life to lead."

CHAPTER FOUR

It's Called Faith

*They are visionaries, not because
they see into the future, but
because they see into the moment.*

A LIFE TO LEAD. You've heard the phrase a thousand times. What does that mean . . . to lead a life? Portrait artists have a trick they use when they are confounded by the familiar. They turn their backs on a painting and view the work through a mirror. The reverse image inevitably reveals subtle flaws in perspective. We think we have lives to lead. But if you pause at any point in your life and look back over your shoulder, you'll discover that we don't lead lives. Our lives lead us.

It is a recurring theme in the story of people in every corner of the world who have given themselves to service. While everyone else is scurrying about in their roles as either planners or players in some grand corporate scheme, there is a whole group of people who approach life differently. They get up every day and involve themselves in the details of living. This day, this moment, they simply give and trust that the rest will take care of itself. They are visionaries, not because they see into the future, but because they see into the moment.

Years before the idea of the *Visionaries* television program was conceived, there was a glimpse at the beauty of this outlook on life. It was in Bolivia.

— ☙ —

A small caravan of old cars lumbers into a little town an hour or so outside of Santa Cruz. It is market day. Through the passenger side window, images bounce by like frames in an old

movie, except these scenes are in color, bright vivid color —
the kind of hues mixed on a pallet loaded with cadmium
orange and lemon yellow with a touch of alizarin crimson.
On the side of the dusty dirt road, groups of women huddle
together behind wooden crates overflowing with fresh-picked
produce. They wear soft-colored skirts, and their long hair
is braided in pigtails. The youngest children cuddle in their
mothers' laps while the older ones race back and forth in front
of the occasional car, then stop on the roadside and watch it
pass as if it were a float in a parade.

Inside the cars are young doctors and nurses who have traveled from the United States to volunteer for two weeks in
a hospital in the city. There, inside a crude operating room,
they perform simple procedures like cleft lip operations, which
would be routine in the developed world, but here, in the
poorest country in South America, they represent a miracle
of monumental proportions. In the Bolivian countryside, the
descendants of the great pre-Columbian societies still believe
that physical deformities are an act of the devil. Children born
with cleft lips are either smothered at birth or are hidden away
for fear the child of the devil will bring harm to the village.

When the medical team arrives in places like Santa Cruz,
missionaries who live and work in the countryside bring the
children out with the hope that an operation will remove this
enormous stigma from the family. The day after the operation,
the child is returned to the village with the gaping split in the
lip miraculously gone. In a few days, the small bandage is removed and the child is led proudly into the village square.
People drop to their knees. The child of the devil has been
touched by the hand of God and is reborn, in the eyes of the
villagers, as a living miracle.

This is all pretty heady stuff for young medical professionals
who are used to working in a modern health care system designed to replace humanism with science. In one of the most
primitive cultures on earth, they witness science transforming
little boys and girls from devils into angels.

In the lead car, a Catholic priest motions the driver to turn
right. Three people are squeezed into the back seat and six

more in each of the two cars that follow. Halfway down the road, the three cars pull over. Doors creak open and the group emerges from the beat-up Toyotas, stretching their cramped limbs. Off to the left, a stark concrete structure sits on a barren lot. In the front of the building is a porch-like enclosure. Standing on the top step is a woman dressed in an azure blue habit with a white veil flowing from her brow down over her shoulders to the middle of her back. She is waiting.

The priest leads the way, and the group, cameras dangling from their necks, follow to the doorstep of the orphanage. Greetings are exchanged, and the nun invites the group with an upturned palm to come inside. It's all part of the experience of traveling with the team. On every trip they take a day off from surgery to go out into the countryside to see how the people live.

Inside, there is a long, dark corridor lit only by the defused light coming through a frosted window at the opposite end of the hall. Children's voices echo out of open doors and dance in the hallway like notes tapped haphazardly on a toy xylophone. Inside one room, seven-, eight-, and nine-year-old boys and girls hover over workbooks spread out on three long wooden tables. The faces of the children sparkle shyly at the sight of the visitors. They have all heard stories of a rich American who visited a long time ago and adopted a child. Some have chairs; most don't. They hold stubby pencils whittled into rough points. But they write ever so softly because they know what will happen during their siesta. The nuns will erase all their words so the books can be used again by another class.

Further down the hall is a dormitory. Wood-framed beds, neatly made up with flowery sheets, are lined up against each wall. Identical small plastic dolls rest against every pillow — every pillow except one. Why, you wonder, does that one child not have a doll? Maybe the little girl has it with her. Maybe there weren't enough to go around.

Around the corner, in a separate wing, is another large room. There are beds in there as well. Instead of dolls against the pillows, there are children with twisted limbs and awful beseeching eyes that seem to cry out from an abyss of mental agony. You look but struggle not to see and then turn around suddenly and walk away.

Outside, the group is milling about shaking their heads in amazement. Some have tears in their eyes. They're crying for the children.

One of the nuns that run the orphanage is standing with her hands folded in front of her, talking with the priest and a few of the other visitors. She says in halting English that she and the other two sisters are from Poland. The children, she explains, are dropped on the doorstep or wander in from the countryside.

You listen with half an ear and look around at the scene. Here, in the middle of nowhere, is this little woman with thin, wire-rimmed glasses feeding, clothing, and educating over a hundred children. You shake your head and look down at her; there is a soft smile on her face that radiates a serenity you can't begin to comprehend. You lean forward, gently pushing your shoulder into the circle of people surrounding her. You have a need to exchange words, to connect in some way with this woman. So you offer a question. "Where do you get the money to support all of these children?"

Her tired eyes are engulfing you as the words land more abruptly than you had intended. Her lips purse together and slowly she turns away. You think that maybe she didn't understand your English, so you ask again. She smiles politely but does not answer. The priest comes to your aid and offers to interpret, so you pose the question one more time. He nods and asks her in Spanish. She draws a breath of resignation and looks up. You catch a hint of embarrassment in the corner of her eyes. Then the words come out in English, slowly but clearly. "I go into the town and I beg."

It's strange how ideas are planted in your mind like saplings in a forest glen. As time passes, the roots burrow deep into the heart of the earth. Above the surface, the tree grows wide and tall but it remains a tree. The forest glen, however, is a clearing in the woods no more. Everything within the shadow of the great tree is shaded by its existence.

The realization that a woman would travel thousands of miles from her home to live in a strange and foreboding land, with no means of support, is awe-inspiring by itself. Add to this her willingness to take on the care of a hundred children, many of whom require so much love, shatters the underpinnings of rationality. Yet, it works. The children have a home, they seem to have enough food, and there is plenty of love echoing in the stark halls.

But the idea, the concept, the fundamental truth that transformed the barren vacant lot in a small Bolivian town into a home for so many children is the same concept behind the Human Service Alliance and it is the same idea that Judy Mayotte lives by.

It's called faith. When you say that word out loud it conjures up religious images, but to many it is simply a belief that there is some unseen force at work. This force reveals itself when we learn to listen to the inner voice and throw care to the winds, thereby letting life take us where it will.

The question that begs to be answered is this: If the secret to happiness is locked away inside an outlook on life that requires us to forget about the outcome and involve ourselves in the daily act of giving, why isn't everyone doing it? The answer is found in the very foundation upon which our entire society is built.

In a modern industrial society, wealth, political power, and military might are all contingent upon the ability of leaders to convince large numbers of people to make individual sacrifices for what is perceived to be the greater good. Whether it be workers in a factory or soldiers on the field of battle, human beings must be persuaded to give up personal liberty and individual needs in exchange for something else.

Where would America be today if the pilgrims of 1620, the patriots of 1776, or the pioneers of the 1840s hadn't refused to accept what their today had to offer and courageously strike out to build a new tomorrow? Ingrained in our psyche is this deep cultural truism that idolizes individuals who refuse to accept the status quo and through the sheer force of will create their own reality.

When we look back through the prism of time at any great historical figure, our vision is obscured by the stories embellished to inspire us to emulate them. Even in modern times we are told to judge the likes of Albert Einstein, Eleanor Roosevelt, and Martin Luther King by the impact they had on future events. The act of retelling their stories plants the idea that there was some grand design to their actions, that the events that followed generations after their deaths were all part of their master plan. This idea has tremendous power and enormous influence because there is much truth to it, although it obscures a fundamental falsehood.

Albert Einstein could no more tame his creative mind than Eleanor Roosevelt could restrain herself from fighting for social justice than Martin Luther King could not speak out about civil rights. Yes, they did accomplish many great deeds, but the irony, of course, is that they achieved fame because, to a certain extent, they weren't thinking about the future; they were living in the here and now.

What does all this have to do with the Polish nun in Bolivia? For that matter, what does it have to do with Judy Mayotte or the volunteers at the Human Service Alliance? The answer is this. From early childhood our culture teaches us to fight for some cause. We are encouraged to battle adversity, overcome obstacles, beat the odds, win the game, earn wealth, and score the most points, all in exchange for a measure of fame sometime in the distant future. Because our purpose in life is to do something difficult and challenging now, so that sometime in the future we will achieve our goal, our lives fall into a pattern of delayed gratification. We live for tomorrow. Our society is built on this concept and many of our great institutions, from sports to industry to religion, depend on sacrifices today for rewards in the future.

The Polish nun in Bolivia, however, lives only for today. She is not taking care of those children so that someday down the road she will get her picture in a magazine. She is doing it because she wants her reward right now. She wants to feel love in her heart today. After all, isn't that the underlying motivation for fame? Don't people want it because they think that it has something to do with love, that if they are famous, people will love them?

The volunteers at the Human Service Alliance prove this point every day. By giving up money and fame, they have discovered an incredible source of happiness in the day-to-day beauty of life.

That does not mean life is a Hallmark card. In fact, one of the hardest lessons to learn is that there is a new depth of happiness that is attainable only when seen from the perspective offered by deep despair. Today Judy Mayotte is working in the State Department as a special advisor in the office that deals with refugee issues. She is living proof that neither of the two ways of life guarantee that it will ever be easy. Her leg hasn't healed as well as the doctors had hoped and she is still unable to use a prosthesis.

Judy Mayotte's approach to life is the same as thousands, maybe millions, of people who have chosen a different outlook, a different perspective on life. They haven't done this because society is evil or because fame is fundamentally abhorrent. They have just come to believe that the cultural system of sacrificing today to achieve happiness later simply doesn't work. There can't be any happiness tomorrow, because as the song says, "When you get there, tomorrow is always a day away."

The great problem that our society confronts today is that the system by which we manufacture fame is beginning to break down. At one time, a monarch could bestow immortality simply by touching a sword to the shoulder of a dutiful soldier and declaring him a knight. Then came modern inventions like the printing press. At first, it served to enhance the power of leaders because the old formulas of creating legends were simply incorporated into new stories and distributed more widely to inspire the populace. But as leaders lost their grip on the dissemination of information, writers and people of independent thought began to use the power of ideas to alter the basic story line and create new idols. With the introduction of mass communication, the power of creating immortality slipped from political leaders into the hands of those who controlled the press. Soon, the power became so intoxicating and hero-making so easy to accomplish that the distinction between notoriety and fame became blurred.

Today, the hero-making machine is so out of control that there is not even the pretense of delineation between the famous and the infamous. Every day... no, virtually every minute, television presents us with yet another character, usually devoid of any human attributes, whose tale is just sordid enough to hold our attention for thirty seconds or so. Then, as if to validate this theater of the absurd, the spoils once bestowed on conquering heroes are handed to a wife-beater because he had his penis cut off or an athlete who commits a violent felony. Only a generation ago, book contracts, movie deals, and five-figure appearance fees were the reward of scholars, statesmen, and artists. Today, well, today it's a different story.

All of this leads to the reason why it is so important to work toward the creation of a new genre of television programing. For better or for worse the television is the campfire around which we gather as a society. It is where we tell our stories, and if history has taught us anything, it is that we eventually become the stories we tell.

One of the stories that needs to be told occurred in Haiti during the economic embargo imposed by the Clinton administration to protest the military overthrow of President Jean-Bertrand Aristide. It was a Saturday afternoon. On the outskirts of Port-au-Prince, there is an old cemetery in a narrow valley between two small hills. Bleached white catacombs, pointing every which way, are squeezed into a gully alongside a dusty dirt road that curls around the burying ground. The dead are entombed above ground in oblong-shaped slabs of concrete separated only by narrow lanes overgrown with scrub brush. A man sits atop one of the tombs with his thin, bony legs dangling over the side. With his left arm he cradles a bundle wrapped in soiled cloth.

Off in the distance a jeep breaks over the hill and descends into the valley. The man looks up for only a brief moment and then turns away and looks back into the morning sky. His back is bent and his shoulders sag under some unseen weight.

The driver of the jeep is a woman. As she passes, she catches a fleeting glimpse of the man out of the corner of her eye. As she downshifts into second gear to begin the climb back out of the valley, the image of the man lingers for a moment.

The man curls the bundle closer to him and lowers his head to shield his face from the cloud of dust that swirls up from the passing jeep. After a moment, he slowly unfolds several layers of cloth and reveals the face of a newborn baby. The child's eyes flicker open in response to the light but then the lids fall slowly shut. The man shakes his head and then pushes his finger against the baby's sunken cheeks trying to elicit a response. There is none.

It was just yesterday that the baby was born in a small village a three-and-a-half-hour drive outside the city. Something went terribly wrong. The young father remembered the screams. He remembered the blood. And he remembered someone handing him the child and telling him his wife was dead. What he could not recall were the hours he walked through the night carrying his only child. The single recollection he retained was the name of a woman who could save his child's life.

Sometime after dawn, he had found his way into the city and began asking where he could find Gladys Sylvestre. Someone directed him to a construction site outside of town where the first children's hospital in the history of the country was being built. He went to the hospital carrying his child whose only source of food was the breast milk of her now dead mother. It was Saturday and no one was working on the building. There was not a soul in sight. He stumbled away, knowing his child was near death. That's when he saw the cemetery in the valley and decided to sit and wait.

The sun was in mid-sky when the same jeep that had passed hours earlier returned over the hill. This time the woman behind the wheel spotted the man as she was descending the hill and wondered what it was he was holding in his arms. She looked closely as she passed and thought to herself that there was something about the scene that seemed odd. She continued on, climbing out of the valley. Once she cleared the hill, she shifted into fourth gear and pushed hard on the accelerator to make as much time as she could on the straightaway. Suddenly, inexplicably, her foot came off the gas pedal and slammed down on the brake. For a moment, she just froze, allowing the jeep to skid sideways to a stop, throwing up a huge cloud of dust that engulfed the jeep. Not knowing why, she then jammed the gear shift into first and yanked the wheel around to head back the way she had come. By the time she began the descent back into the valley, she was already feeling a bit foolish. Nonetheless, she pulled the vehicle over across from the cemetery, jumped out, and walked deliberately up to the man sitting on top of the tomb.

He seemed not to notice her approach and did not look up from his slouch until she was standing in front of him.

"Excuse me," the woman said, "but do you mind telling me what you're doing here?"

The man blinked away whatever thoughts were consuming his consciousness and looked into the woman's face. He answered in a dull monotone that made his voice seem as if it were coming from some far-off place. "I've come looking for Gladys Sylvestre."

The woman did not answer, but just looked at him with an expression that appeared to be as amazed as it was confused.

"They told me back in my village that she could take care of my baby. My wife is dead. I have no way to feed my baby . . . no one to take care of her. I must work to live. . . . " His voice trailed off.

The woman reached into his arms and peeled back the blankets covering the child, listening as the man continued. "I went to the hospital but there was no one there. Then I

Gladys Sylvestre and young charge at the orphan hospital in Haiti.

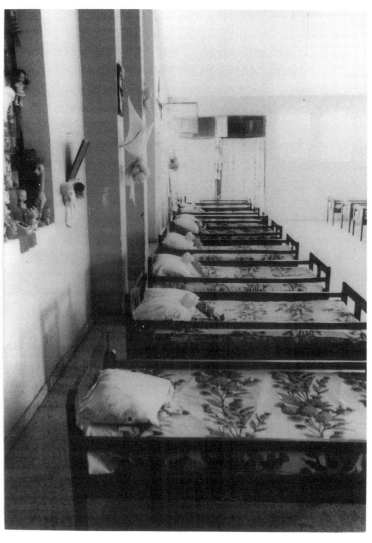

Orphaned children are greeted by a clean bed and a loving touch in their new home.

saw the cemetery and I thought...I thought, well, at least I could...."

The woman lifted one of the child's eyelids with her thumb and then looked into the man's face and said, "I'm Gladys Sylvestre."

Gladys Sylvestre was born in a small village outside Port-au-Prince to a poor family. When she was twelve years old, she moved to the city to live with an older sister so she could attend school. One day she met a woman from the United States who had no children of her own. She offered to take Gladys to America and help her to get an education.

There was never any question in her mind that she would someday return to her homeland. While in the United States, she studied nursing with the vague idea that it would provide her with a skill that would be helpful when she returned home. While out of the country, she met and married a Haitian man who also had been helped by a caring American. He too wanted to learn skills that would make it possible to return home and have an impact on the poverty gripping the country.

In 1980, they returned together when he accepted a position with World Vision, an international relief organization. Today, he heads all of the organization's work in Haiti.

Gladys was immediately struck with an odd form of culture shock. Although she was born and had lived the early years of her life in the country, the poverty seemed horribly more vivid. She immediately began sheltering children abandoned on the streets in her home. She volunteered with community groups and offered her nursing skills in clinics set up inside Cité Soleil, the massive slum that houses thousands of people.

One day she found a four-month-old child who had been left on the street by his mentally retarded mother. The baby had received severe burns, and as Gladys nursed him back to health she decided to commit her first major act of irrevocable charity. She adopted the child. She found that there was something strangely liberating in just doing what needed to be done and trusting that it would all work out in the end.

Almost immediately, another opportunity presented itself. One weekend shortly after Gladys had taken her new baby home, the phone rang. She was on the first floor and her husband was upstairs. They both picked up an extension at the same time. On the other end of the line was the pastor of their church. He didn't waste any time getting to the point. There were children that needed help. The story that unfolded was about an American woman who had come to Haiti, apparently with good intentions of helping the children orphaned on the streets. She opened an orphanage and took in dozens of children. Apparently overwhelmed by the magnitude of the job she had undertaken, the woman fled the country. She left behind a building in which one large room housed dozens of children, many of whom were infants, who now had no food and were wallowing in their own excrement.

Even while retelling the story twelve years later, Gladys seems amazed at the succession of unplanned events that charted the course of her life.

"I told this man I was going to check with my husband to see if I could really go and help the children. I didn't even have to go upstairs. I heard him on the phone line saying, 'Oh, Gladys, I think you're really going to like this kind of work, you should do it.'

"At that point, I wondered if that was really my husband or was that God who said, 'You wanted an orphanage, you got it. I'm giving it to you in the worst shape so you can see how miracles happen.' At that point, I felt maybe I couldn't do what I should do because I didn't have the means. I had asked God to give me children that I could care for, and somehow this was an answer to my prayers. And blindly, after arguing with myself, I closed my eyes and, as a step of faith, I said I was going to take over the orphanage and see what I could do for the children."

The "step of faith" as she called it seemed to set off a chain of events that never could have been predicted or planned.

When a need arose, somehow resources arrived. In the beginning, the needs were so great and the work so overwhelming that just getting through the day required all the energy a person could muster. She did not have time to think too much about the future. Maybe it was more out of necessity than overwhelming faith, but she developed a style that concentrated on the immediate needs while leaving herself open and alert for signals that might be guiding her way.

"I feel like God has picked me out of a group of people and said, 'I want you to be open. Just stand there and be like a feather or a cloud. Anything can go through them, because they're very light. And that's all I need you to be. You don't have to worry; you don't have to question why.'"

Enmeshed as she was in the demands of the moment, her perspective on life gave a clarity and purity to issues that in another context might have seemed overwhelmingly difficult to tackle. As she was rebuilding the orphanage on a new concept that organized the children into family units, new challenges emerged almost immediately.

The children needed to be educated, so she started a school that would serve children in the neighborhood as well as the children in the orphanage. This, she thought, would solve two immediate needs: educating the children and breaking down the walls of the orphanage so that the parentless children could interact with children from the community who came from traditional Haitian homes.

As parents began to bring their children into the school, she became aware of the needs of the community around the orphanage. Children and parents often arrived with obvious medical problems. Gladys started a clinic on the grounds of the orphanage.

Out of nowhere, in ways she never could have foreseen, people arrived to help. She told friends from the United States about her work and some responded with donations and others came as volunteers to help. A producer from Hollywood heard about her work and began championing her cause, shipping supplies and spreading the word.

News of the miracles occurring behind the orphanage walls

began to spread around Port-au-Prince as well. Soon children, some only a day or two old, began arriving on her doorstep. They presented a new challenge. Newborns not only required more care; they needed more love in the form of one-on-one attention than a group home could provide. Gladys, once again, made decisions to address the immediate need. She found a vacant home in the city and turned the bedrooms into a nursery for the children, many of whom required medical attention. Then she set about the task of finding permanent homes for the babies.

It seemed that every time Gladys made what she called a "step of faith," resources arrived. First, however, she needed to take the step, to make the passage from the security of the known into a realm of uncertainty. It was within this single act that she found the magic. She simply walked into the unknown.

"Love is to cast out the fear, and when you do that, you will realize that what you had in your heart was right. I've never feared anything. And people always ask, 'What's next, Gladys?' I always have nexts...I have a lot of nexts."

When she began taking in newborn children, she had absolutely no idea how she would feed them, how she would find the money for their medicine, or even how she would pay the rent on the building that housed the nursery. No need stirs the world to action like the cry of an abandoned child, however, and out of nowhere people appeared to adopt the children filling the nursery that Gladys named the Rainbow of Love Nursery.

She could not have known it at the time, but with each adoption the groundwork was being laid for a project that would occur nearly a decade later. In the beginning, the opportunity to place abandoned children in homes outside of Haiti solved two immediate problems. First, it ensured that the child would have the love and affection he or she needed from a young age. The second benefit was that couples throughout North America and Europe offered to donate funds to the orphanage to cover the cost of facilitating the adoption and to help support the children who could not be adopted because of their age or because of their health. Over time, however, something more powerful began to build.

A strange and wonderful pattern began to develop. A family in Ontario would hear about Gladys somehow. They would travel to Haiti and adopt a child. The new family would tell their story to friends and family and before long, another childless couple would come forward and ask about their experience. Soon, they were connected with Gladys. Over the years, more than five hundred Haitian children moved into communities all over the world. These families networked together to raise money for Gladys and to make regular pilgrimages to Haiti as volunteers. One of those children who went out into the world to act as an ambassador for Gladys was the baby she found in the cemetery.

Later, when someone came to Gladys and told her that there was a room inside the General Hospital in which children were living in deplorable conditions, she had the resources to act. Down a dark corridor in an unlit room, she found twenty-two profoundly retarded and severely disabled children. One child, whose mouth was contorted open, had been neglected for so long that flies had laid eggs inside his mouth. On April 5, 1994, Gladys and two dozen volunteers arrived at the General Hospital in a caravan of cars. They marched down the hall, scooped up the children, and carried them out to the waiting cars. They were taken to a two-story, three-bedroom home that Gladys rented with money donated by supporters outside the country. There they were given baths, new clothes, and clean beds. Today the children receive 'round-the-clock care by a staff who genuinely care about their well-being.

The handicapped children were not the only patients that Gladys rescued out of the General Hospital. It was a place that seemed to swallow children alive. They would come in with injuries or an ailment that required no more than a quick fix and died because there were not enough resources to go around. Over and over again, she found children wandering the halls with life-threatening diseases or injuries that required only a little attention.

The only answer was the creation of the first children's hospital in the history of the country. The problem, of course, was that she had no money, no land, no medical equipment. She had only one thing going for her. She had faith.

CHAPTER FIVE

Circles of Giving

*The magic occurred at the points of
connection, where lives intersected.*

VISIONARIES began in the winter of 1992 when a single-page letter was typed into a personal computer in the loft of a nineteenth-century granite building on Commercial Wharf along Boston's waterfront. It was just four paragraphs long and only two copies were mailed: one to the *Non-Profit Times* and the other to the *Chronicle of Philanthropy*. The brief press release announced that a producer in Boston was putting together a television series that "explores the magic that occurs when one human being helps another." Non-profit organizations were invited to apply to be included in the new series.

At the time, there was not a single dollar in funding and no corporation, foundation, or television network had committed to support the idea. The producer had no equipment, no crew, and, more importantly, no clue about how it was all going to happen. There was just a vague sense of throwing the idea into the wind and waiting to see what would happen.

A short time later, the phone rang. Someone on the other end of the line said that they had read a two-sentence blurb on the front page of the *Non-Profit Times* about a television show called *Visionaries*. How could they get an application to be included? The phone didn't stop ringing for two years. Hundreds of organizations from all over the country either read the brief notice in the *Non-Profit Times* or a later article in the *Chronicle of Philanthropy* or heard about it from someone else. Amnesty International, Goodwill Industries, CARE, and UNICEF called to request applications. A public relations official from the United States Olympic Committee read about it on a plane. He called from the airport during a layover to pitch a story on members of his board of fundraisers.

Soon, thick packets started arriving in the mail. Accompanying their application forms, organizations sent along copies of their annual reports, newsletters, newspaper clippings, and video tapes showing their work. There were coffee mugs, key chains, calendars, and complimentary note cards; one organization sent in a T-shirt criss-crossed with painted tire marks produced by people in wheelchairs.

Most of the application packets told remarkable stories of people in every walk of life who had found a way to fulfill a mysterious urge to serve. There was the three-inch-thick bundle of information from a woman by the name of Gina Burns who lives in Chapel Hill, North Carolina. She operates an organization out of her living room called the Group B-Strep Association. You probably have never heard of Group B-Strep, and that is precisely the point. Though this bacteria is the most common cause of life-threatening infections in newborn babies, even many doctors didn't know that 15 to 35 percent of all women carry it, resulting in the death of two thousand babies every year. Many more of the twelve thousand infected babies will suffer brain damage or other birth defects, most of which are preventable.

In 1989, Gina Burns and her husband lost their baby to the bacteria, which is passed from the mother to the infant during childbirth. In just four years, with no paid staff and virtually no budget, they built a support group of parents, doctors, and medical researchers that now has five thousand members.

They have convinced national medical associations to issue bulletins and have stimulated a national debate regarding the screening of pregnant women. They have supported research at Harvard University Medical School, and now the development of a vaccine seems imminent. Every day, four or five newborns die of bacteria that have been around for centuries, but no one seemed to care until Gina Burns began speaking out. Now the most powerful forces in the medical community are hailing her as a visionary. It would take almost two years to find the funding for the episode on Gina Burns.

One of the packets included a homemade photo album with handwritten captions that portrayed the work of a small organization called SHARE. The acronym stands for Society for Hospital and Resource Exchange.

The group, headed by New York physician Martha M. MacGuffie, acquires the services of volunteers and collects donated equipment with the goal of delivering services to one of the most unusual places on the earth. It is an island located in the middle of Lake Victoria in Kenya. It is the largest lake on earth, and the island is the home of twelve thousand inhabitants who have the highest infant mortality rate in the world; nine out of every ten already have malaria.

Archeologists think this may be the place where human life began, but today it is one of the most medically deprived populations anywhere. At least it was until Dr. MacGuffie came along. They have built a clinic, immunized thousands, and instituted an array of life-saving programs on the island and throughout the surrounding area. Hundreds, if not thousands, of lives are being saved every year by the group of American doctors, while a full 100 percent of every dollar contributed to this organization goes to services.

Mixed in with the four-color brochures and fancy presentation packets from some of the largest and most influential organizations in the country were stories about people like Sam Ross, who started an organization forty-six years ago called Green Chimneys. The name comes from the color of the chimneys on the farm he persuaded his father to purchase for him when he was only nineteen years old. Over the years, he has built it into one of the most successful residential treatment facilities for emotionally disturbed and physically abused children in the country. The entire program operates on a single concept: When children leave one of the boroughs of New York and arrive on the 150-acre functioning farm, they are immediately each placed in charge of an animal. It could be an injured bald eagle or a new calf; it does not matter. What matters is for the first time in these children's lives, another living thing is depending on them for survival. It is from that single relationship that all therapy evolves.

A vivid picture began to emerge that revealed the size and breadth of the non-profit world and the odd relationship America has with one of the most integral aspects of its society.

The big picture is that there are over 1.2 million non-profit organizations incorporated in the United States and working in virtually every country on earth. Over 14 million Americans work as paid employees or serve as regular volunteers for these groups. They comprise a full 20 percent of the service economy of the country and 7 percent of the Gross National Product. Philanthropic organizations spend $390 billion a year and control $800 billion in assets.

That having been said, it must be recognized that measuring the influence of the non-profit world by quoting dollar figures is a little bit like determining the beauty of a cloud by calculating its weight. What makes it special and so mysterious is not what you can grasp, but what slips through your fingers.

The world of philanthropy is an ever-changing montage of moving images that eludes definition, or even understanding, in the same way the universe we see on a starlit night defies comprehension. The problem is that the units of measurement we use aren't measurements at all, but concepts that stretch our imagination to the limit. Our minds can no more visualize the distance between stars in terms of light years than we can quantify acts of charity in units of love.

We try, nonetheless. Every year, business-oriented publications like *Fortune* and *Money Magazine* run cover stories on the top charities in the country. It's a contest. Whoever collects the most money wins. But you can't judge non-profit organizations on market criteria any more than you can score a tennis match in touchdowns. Therefore, when the applications for inclusion in *Visionaries* started spilling out of the cardboard boxes into piles on the floor, new units of measure needed to be found.

Since no one has yet invented a meter to measure degrees of love, a broad set of criteria was established as a starting point. First, the presence of an identifiable individual visionary was a prerequisite — not because the goal was to find unsung heroes and bestow on them the mantle of fame. Quite the opposite: a basic theme was to demonstrate the rewards of serving in anonymity. The individual visionary, however, was an essential tool in the construction of a new approach to documentary television.

Traditionally, documentary television has confined itself to the dissemination of facts. As a result, we often see powerful images de-emotionalized by cold words uttered by a disinterested narrator or a benign correspondent who dominates the screen and interprets every scene.

On the opposite end of the non-fiction spectrum is what has become known as reality programing. This approach takes the shortest and easiest route to the lowest gut emotion. The technique is to ride on fear to reach anger; on topics like governmental reform, the goal is to stir indignation into outrage; and on myriad social issues, pity is peddled in the hope of a guilt-ridden response. The essential point of departure between *Visionaries* and what has been done before was in the middle of the two. But — and this is a big but — the formula is not found in a mixture of the two. A measure of facts stirred together with a dose of fear and a cupful of anger does not get you *Visionaries*. It gets you *America's Most Wanted*.

The goal from the very beginning was to travel atop a whole different set of emotions with the hope of arriving at a new place not often visited by television. The vehicle needed to get there was shared experience. That is why the individual visionaries were important because they would serve as the viewer's companions, the persons through whom the viewer would feel what it is like to be in a refugee camp in Sudan or in an orphanage in Haiti.

A second component that was considered essential in the selection process was that the organization's work present an opportunity for the viewer to witness the actual act of giving. Many, if not most, of the organizations that applied to be in the series were involved in important and inspiring work, but what they actually did was far removed from the physical act of one person helping another.

Gifts in Kind, generally considered to be one of the most

effective and efficient organizations in the country, submitted an application, and their president, Susan Corrigan, came to Boston to talk about their work. Gifts in Kind is always listed in business publications as one of the most efficient non-profits because an extraordinarily high percentage of what it receives in donations goes back out in the form of services. It receives donated material, equipment and services from large corporations and redistributes them to other non-profits. These groups, in turn, use the computers, office equipment, and even transportation services to help them operate more efficiently and ultimately to use a higher percentage of their donations to help people.

As much of an impact as this kind of work can have, the nature of the service does not lend itself to emotion-evoking television. Nonetheless, an important discovery can be made in the story of Gifts in Kind and the many other organizations that play a largely administrative role in the world of giving. If you are truly trying to find a method to gauge the impact of a given organization, an essential unit of measurement might be the amount and degree of connection it facilitates.

Isn't that what it is all about? People connecting with people. The lesson of the Human Service Alliance was the depth or the degree to which one human being can connect with another. When you reduce Judy Mayotte's work and the role of advocacy to its lowest common denominator, you discover that it is essential to connect people on opposite ends of the human spectrum.

This all leads to a third criteria that was used in the selection of programs to profile. In addition to there being an identifiable visionary and a story that showed the actual delivery of services, organizations that offered a unique opportunity to explore the deeper issues like the power of human connection were placed in the pile of finalists.

One such story began in the most unlikely of places: in a smoke-filled room at the Democratic convention on Au-

gust 16, 1956. The previous night the name of Adlai Stevenson had been placed in nomination by a handsome young
senator from Massachusetts. The crowd had gone wild. Suddenly, a wave of support rolled across the convention floor to
nominate Senator John Fitzgerald Kennedy as the Democratic
candidate for vice-president. Anarchy erupted within delegations representing states with large Catholic constituencies.
Within hours, open revolt was occurring in a number of cau-
cus rooms where Kennedy supporters were rallying delegates
to dump Estes Kefauver in exchange for the dynamic young
war hero.

Behind the scenes, Kennedy operatives under the direction
of the candidate's brother Bobby fanned out to keep the fires
burning as the critical vote approached. In one such room,
the Ohio delegation was in the midst of raucous debate when
Kennedy aide Kenny O'Donnell took up a position at the
back of the room. He must have liked what he saw. Catholic
delegates, swept up in a tide of emotion, seemed to have captured the moment, if not the hearts of their fellow Ohioans.
Suddenly, a young congressional aide jumped up on a chair
and with one foot perched on a table called for the crowd's
attention. The clamor subsided and the group listened.

The man's name was Gene Krizek. He called on his fellow
delegates to remember that they had made a solemn commitment to vote on the first ballot for Kefauver. He captured
their attention by hammering away at the issue of loyalty but
sensed that he was not winning any votes. Then he changed
his tack. "Besides," the young Ohioan said, "let's be honest.
We all know that Eisenhower is going to win this election. Do
you really want to nominate a man who could be the future
of this party, knowing he will go down to certain defeat? It
could ruin his career. Let's live by our commitment to vote
for Kefauver on the first ballot, then look to Kennedy in four
years."

Kenny O'Donnell turned and walked out of the room. A
little while later, the Ohio delegation cast their votes for
Kefauver, who went on to join Adlai Stevenson on the presidential ticket to face Eisenhower and Nixon in the November

election. O'Donnell approached Gene Krizek on the convention floor shortly after the vote. He led the younger man to a room overlooking the convention floor where Kennedy was sequestered with aides.

As the senator approached, he stretched out his hand toward Krizek, and with the wry smile that was his trademark, said, "So, you're the young fella that's so interested in my future."

Krizek laughed and took hold of the future president's hand and pledged his support. Kennedy responded, "I hope you will be as loyal to me in the future as you have been to Kefauver in the past."

Loyalty was a commodity that had been ingrained in Gene Krizek long ago — not as an abstract concept, but as an absolute article of faith that required unswerving commitment regardless of the consequences. His father, who immigrated to the United States from Czechoslovakia at the age of fourteen, demonstrated the depth of that commitment. In his new home, he prospered as a successful businessman. In 1914, however, his native country, Bohemia, then a part of the Hungarian Empire, was overrun by the Germans prior to the U.S. entrance into World War I. Feeling the call of his country in its time of need, he wrestled with the conflicting loyalties of his adopted home and the place where he was born. He chose to give up the security of his now comfortable life in the United States and joined the French army. He was assigned to a division of Czech legionnaires and sent into battle. After the war, he wanted to build the new Democratic Republic of Czechoslovakia before returning to his family in the United States.

In the wake of the foreign war, a sense of fervent isolationism was sweeping across the country. Congress reacted by terminating the citizenship of anyone who fought on behalf of a foreign nation. Gene Krizek's father became a man without a country. He embarked on a campaign to win back the citizenship of all the men who had fought America's common enemy while serving in the ranks of allied armies. He was elected president of the new national organization of legionnaires and spoke around the country to veterans groups, often with his son at his side.

It was in these smoky legion halls filled with boisterous men bonded together by having shared in war the most profound of human experiences that the young Krizek learned the power of connecting in a common cause. It took many years to tear down the walls of prejudice built by the isolationists, but finally, with the election of a Democratic president, Franklin Delano Roosevelt, the honor of Gene Krizek's father was restored.

By then, however, the Depression had hit and wiped out the family's savings. Too proud to declare bankruptcy, the father took a job as a salesman, determined to pay back every penny he owed. Then, at the age of forty-four, he was felled by cancer. Gene Krizek, at the age of fourteen, became the man of the family. His mother, saddled by the lingering debt, went to work in a defense plant. Gene helped to support his seven-year-old twin brother and sister with a paper route and whatever odd jobs he could find. One of his most vivid memories was obtaining a special permit to drive the family car at the age of fourteen so he could get his mother to work every day. After school, he would take care of his brother and sister, clean the house, and cook the meals for the family, while managing to do well enough in his studies to be named valedictorian of his high school class in 1946.

In the years between high school and the Democratic convention of 1956, Gene Krizek completed two tours of duty in the Air Force. The first came after finishing his first year of college during the last days of World War II. The second came when he interrupted his education once again to serve during the Korean War. He became active in Democratic politics, and after his military service went to Washington as an aide to Ohio Congressman Charles A. Varnik. He was in his office on Capitol Hill just a few months after the 1956 election when he got a call from John Kennedy's brother-in-law, Steve Smith, asking if he would help to build a Kennedy organization. Krizek went to work doing what he did best: connecting people in a common cause. He created an organization of congressional staffers committed to Kennedy. Every building on Capitol Hill had a captain, and on every floor there was a lieutenant who organized workers in each office.

Within these offices were not only the aides to congressmen and senators from all over the country, but the staff of congressional committees. These volunteers possessed the expertise and the factual data on virtually every economic, social, and military issue confronting the country. When the young candidate needed a fact or a figure or a full-length position paper on taxes, education reform, or the number of bushels of rice exported by Laos, it was only a phone call away.

On election night in November 1959, Gene Krizek was in Seattle as Kennedy's state coordinator, having spent the later months of the campaign trying to organize the state of Washington. It was his unenviable job to call Hyannisport and report to Bobby Kennedy that their last-ditch effort to pull out the state had failed. On the other end of the line, the future attorney general could hardly hear Krizek's report because of the crowd cheering the returns from other states. Bobby Kennedy asked Krizek to hold on because someone wanted to talk to him.

"Hey, Gene," the voice yelled into the phone. "This is Jack. Hey, Gene, I understand you have an interest in foreign affairs," Kennedy's voice dripped with sarcasm. "Geez, Gene, I'm going to be looking for a secretary of state, but I don't see how I can give you that job. I mean, Gene, you lost Washington." Both men laughed.

Three months later, Gene Krizek was working for the White House as the president's liaison with the State Department. The irony was overwhelming. Gene Krizek, the son of a man who lost his citizenship because of his interaction with a foreign country, became the connection between the White House and the governmental agency responsible for maintaining contact with every foreign country on earth.

After the assassination of President Kennedy, Gene Krizek was called into a meeting at the White House with Lyndon Johnson, the new president, and asked to remain through the next administration. It would be more than two decades before he would leave government, serving Democratic and Republican administrations as the director of the State Department's Office of Congressional Liaison. During the closing days of Jimmy Carter's administration, he began to consider moving on, to find a new challenge that would combine his love of foreign affairs with his knowledge of government.

Throughout all of his years in Washington, his wife, Addy, and their three children had been active in one community organization after another. She had worked as director of the Red Cross, served on the board of Friendship House, and was the president of the local chapter of the Juvenile Diabetes Foundation. He was active in international causes related to his work in the State Department on behalf of refugees. In 1975, he was given a presidential commendation for shepherding through Congress the Indochinese Refugee Act, which helped save the lives of thousands of boat people stranded on the high seas. This work led to his appointment as consulting development director of Georgetown University's Center for Immigration and Refugee Assistance, which worked with programs throughout Africa, Asia, and Latin America.

Then, in 1985, an opportunity presented itself. Gene was serving on the international board of directors of the Juvenile Diabetes Foundation with a friend who owned a successful direct mail fundraising company. When they got together for fundraising meetings, they would often talk about the problems confronting governments in whatever political hot spot happened to be in the news. One day, the friend said, "You know, Gene, you ought to start your own non-profit organization. You've been all over the world with the State Department. You know what works and what doesn't."

Something about the idea struck a nerve. It was true. He did know what worked and what didn't. Most of all, he believed that many of the problems America was having in its efforts to fight poverty at home and to help developing countries were because we still hadn't learned an essential truth revealed by many of the programs that came out of the Kennedy administration. He had seen the young idealistic recruits going overseas under the auspices of programs like the

Peace Corps, believing that they could solve the problems of the world. But when he traveled around the globe escorting congressional delegations, he came to the realization that America did not have all the answers. It seemed that its view of other nations and poor people in general was often based on a perspective of arrogance and an assumption that because we are a wealthy country, we must have all the answers.

Out of this knowledge grew the rough outline for an organization that would work to unite people in a common quest. It couldn't be about hand-outs; it must be about giving people a hand up. It almost didn't matter what the challenge happened to be. What mattered was that whatever project was undertaken, it be a joint endeavor based on the principle of shared resources. Yes, America as a nation was wealthy, but it didn't have all the answers. The concept was to combine the wealth of the developed world with the ideas and labor of those who lived and worked in the areas that needed help.

At the age of fifty-six, Gene Krizek decided it was time to start a whole new life. His friend, the direct mail expert, agreed to help raise the money, and Gene's wife and their three sons volunteered to do whatever needed to be done. The question was, however, what needed to be done?

Then, one night, Gene Krizek was at home nodding in front of the television. They had just signed up for cable television and he had been surfing through the channels when he came across a rerun of a movie starring Robby Benson. It was called *Running Brave* and was the story of Olympic gold medalist Billy Mills. Mills had won a stunning upset at the 1964 games in Tokyo by beating the world record holder in the 10,000-meter run. What caught Gene Krizek's attention was the story of how Mills, whose mother was a full-blooded Lakota Sioux, was raised in poverty on Pine Ridge Indian Reservation. Gene sat upright on the couch and yelled for his wife to come in and watch the story. It was one of those events that never could have been planned. The next day, Gene Krizek called every person he could think of who might know how to get in touch with the man who had won an Olympic gold medal two decades earlier. Finally, he tracked down Billy Mills in Califor-

Gene Krizek, founder of Christian Relief Services, works the food distribution line at the Appalachia food pantry.

Billy Mills, member of the Lakota tribe and Olympic gold medalist, returned to the land of his birth to make a difference in the lives of his fellow Native Americans.

nia, where he was living the life of a successful motivational speaker who had never lost contact with his roots. They met, and it was decided that the new non-profit organization being formed by Gene Krizek would start work in one of the poorest "Third World" locations on earth, the Pine Ridge Indian Reservation.

It was a critical first step because it firmly established the central philosophy of the organization that was named Christian Relief Services and put in place a system by which Gene Krizek could do what he did best: connect people in a common cause.

Working on Indian reservations has been the undoing of countless charities that went to places like Pine Ridge in South Dakota or Slim Butte in Montana with the idea that they were going to save the destitute Native Americans by delivering an array of services. The new organization started with a different approach. They went onto the reservation with Billy Mills with the idea of learning rather than teaching. The only question that was asked was, How can we work together?

The answer was water. In places like the 28-million-acre Pine Ridge Reservation, the rivers were polluted by uranium mines operated by non-Indians outside the reservation, and well water was far too deep to be accessed by traditional methods. Water was a critical resource for both practical and deep spiritual reasons. Without water, a traditional Native American family was disconnected from Mother Earth because it could not survive off the land.

The solution to the problem seemed to be simple enough; bring in sophisticated well-drilling equipment and start to work. But the answer was far more complicated, and simply drilling wells would constitute a hand-out rather than a hand up. On a deeper level, the team of volunteers assembled by Christian Relief Services began to understand, with the help of Billy Mills and the people who lived on the reservation, that nothing would work if the philosophy behind the work was not based on traditional Indian ways.

One of the recurring symbols in Native American culture is the circle. There is a deep belief that all living things are

connected in a spiritual world and that life's failures are at-
tributable to breaks in the circle. Charitable giving to Indian
reservations has consistently failed to recognize this point, and
instead of a circle of giving, what often results is a cycle of
hand-outs that serves only to rob the people whom the gift is
intended to help of their dignity and self-esteem.

Drilling wells, therefore, could work only if the act was part
of a larger, circuitous program designed to dignify the entire
human experience. The effort began with a letter mailed to
thousands of people around the United States. Those who
responded were individuals who for some reason connected
with the desire to help. This desire, in the form of a donation, purchased two items: well-drilling services and seeds to
grow crops. Once the wells were drilled, the people who donated money for that purpose had their name placed on the
well and received information about the people who would
benefit from their gift. Many contributors actually traveled to
the Indian reservation and visited the family, completing the
circle of giving in an even more profound way.

On the reservation the families who received the gift of water participated in the construction of the wells and, in many
cases, received seeds and farming supplies from fellow Native
Americans who operated a CRS-supported program to encourage and train small farmers. With the seeds they planted
small family gardens nourished with the water from the well.
The food from this garden was a byproduct of the original gift,
but was made possible by the hard work of the family themselves. This hard work and the resultant produce completed
the circle of giving by instilling a sense of pride and dignity in
the family that was now living off the land in total harmony
with the spiritual teaching of its people.

Because CRS recognized the importance of keeping the
circle active, they regularly updated contributors with information about how their donation was being used, resulting
in a steady flow of resources. By 1994 over two hundred water wells had been constructed and fifteen thousand packets
of vegetable seed were being distributed every year on just
one of the twenty-five reservations CRS now works. Today

they operate more programs and deliver more resources to Indian reservations than any other private charity in the country. Many of these programs are aimed at instilling a sense of dignity in young Native Americans by supporting youth camps, athletic programs, schools, and even shelters for battered women and children. All of these are founded and operated by Native Americans.

Slowly, the circles of giving began to take on a three-dimensional form, like a globe being orbited by thousands of rings, each spinning on a different axis. The magic occurred at the points of connection, where lives intersected. When one sphere of charity touched another, it seemed to ignite the creation of a third. Billy Mills, for example, ran into an old friend at an Olympic event. His name was Kip Keino; he was the first African gold medalist and won an assortment of medals at both the 1968 and 1972 games. In his entire life Kip had earned only $20,000 from running. That money had come from a professional tour twenty years earlier. He had taken the money and purchased a piece of land and a small two bedroom home in his native Kenya. He and his wife, a registered nurse, immediately began taking in orphaned children. When Kip Keino and Billy Mills met again in the 1980s, he had sixty-eight children in his home and had already raised and sent off into the world another hundred. Billy Mills introduced Kip Keino to Gene Krizek, and before long letters were going out around the United States. New circles of support were revolving to educate the children and to equip and run the functioning farm that would someday provide all the food and most of the cash needed to make Kip Keino's Children's Home self-sufficient.

Soon over a half million people from every walk of life all across the United States were making small contributions to CRS, nearly 90 percent of which went directly into programs like community gardens in Appalachia, well-drilling in Ethiopia, and a Native American arts and crafts program.

A major part of the effort revolved around the idea of bringing more and more individuals into the circle by leveraging the cash contributions with the in-kind donations of others. The small cash gifts of individual donors were used to pay the cost of transporting nearly a million dollars in medicine, medical equipment, and food to a hospital in Poland. All told, over $15 million in clothing, food, medical supplies, and just about every kind of building material imaginable was collected and stored in warehouses. Individual donors helped pay the cost of storage and shipping the relief to places in every region of the world. Plumbing supplies helped bring water to twenty-five thousand people in Uganda. Surgical supplies were delivered to cancer patients in Slovakia. Sewing machines arrived in Peru, helping poor villagers once reliant on the rain forest to earn a living.

It all happened as if by magic. First, there would be a phone call, sometimes followed by a site visit or a meeting. Then a letter would go out and thousands of people would respond.

One day Gene Krizek got a call from a woman who was in the United States for a short visit. She said she was in New York and would like to take the train down to Washington to tell him about a project with which she needed help. The next day, a young black woman entered his office. Her small, thin body exuded a spontaneous energy. She boldly walked up to him, took hold of his outstretched hand, and said, "Hello, Mr. Krizek. My name is Gladys Sylvestre, and I want you to help me build a hospital for the children of Haiti."

It was the ultimate intersection of two vibrant arcs of giving. Inside Gladys's sphere there were hundreds of people connected together by their adopted children. They and their friends had access to tens of thousands of dollars in donated building materials and medical equipment. What they needed was someone to collect and store the goods. Then the biggest task of all was to get them into the country. Since President Aristide had been driven from office, there was an economic embargo. Building material did not fall under the humanitarian relief exemption that allowed food and medicine into the country.

Gene Krizek set about doing what he did best. He formed the connection. First, he opened his warehouse doors to all of Gladys Sylvestre's supporters and connected them with his own contributors through a mailing that asked for the resources to deliver these donations to Haiti. All along, he had been using his expertise in government to facilitate the shipment of emergency aid into war zones and areas of famine; now he had to pull out all the stops to do what no one thought possible: build the first children's hospital in the history of Haiti, during the middle of a highly publicized embargo.

As the concrete mix, floor tile, windows, and doors started arriving at the CRS warehouse, Gene Krizek worked the halls of government, finally arriving at a windowless room at the State Department in Washington. There, he told Gladys's story to two stone-faced officials whose mission in life was to strangle Haiti's dictatorial leadership into submission. In the end, however, the story was all too powerful and a special exception was granted. And once again, another circle was completed.

CHAPTER SIX

Choosing to Give

*Life is not about how we master
the world; it's about what we
construct out of the circumstances
that are beyond our control.*

THE HISTORY of our species is little more than a chronicle of how our lives have intersected at times and in places that no one could have predicted. But we live every day under the spell of our egos, which masterfully weaves threads of chance into whole cloth, all the while convincing us that the fabric of our lives is a creation of our own making. Life is not about how we master the world; it's about what we construct out of the circumstances that are beyond our control.

Visionaries, therefore, are not people who have the ability to determine the future. They are individuals who have been at the intersection — people who have felt the awesome power of these unforeseen events and been swept into the primordial flow that is that raw material of life.

Such an event occurred on the night of July 25, 1993, in a small Minnesota town called Eagan. It was a Saturday night. Randy Nellis, the manager of a local restaurant, had spent most of the evening with his wife, Vicki, at a nearby hospital. She had been experiencing pains in her stomach for over a week and they decided to go to the emergency room to make sure it was nothing serious. After some routine tests, they drove to the home of Vicki's mother, who had been taking care of their two-year-old daughter.

Now it's after midnight and the Nellis family is heading home. The headlights from Randy's blue 1989 Cavalier are boring through the cool summer night as he drives along a familiar road just two miles from their small apartment. Trees line the right side of the road. On the left, single family homes sit in dark pockets illuminated only by an occasional lamp set atop a lawn post.

It's quiet inside the car. Randy's face is lit by the cold green glow from the instrument panel, where the speedometer needle hovers between thirty and thirty-five miles an hour. His wife is staring straight ahead in a weary gaze. She has been in a lot of pain for days and still doesn't know why. Curled up in her lap is her little girl. She's sleeping quietly with her thumb in her mouth and soft wisps of her strawberry blond hair covering her furrowed brow. She's wearing a light blue blouse with a picture of Big Bird embroidered on the front. Her name is Ashley, and she is a "daddy's girl."

A thousand miles away in the state of Connecticut another young family is feeling the weariness of a long day. Dan and Laura Grasso also have a two-year-old. His name is Vinny. He is spending his first night in the new home the family had spent a year and a half waiting to be built.

Unassembled furniture leans against freshly painted walls. The refrigerator is empty, and paper bags overflowing with the contents of dresser drawers are strewn everywhere. Cardboard boxes stuffed with clothes are stacked in a corner of the master bedroom. There are no curtains on the windows. Dan, who works for the local power company, has collapsed on the bed after spending most of the day working to grade and seed the front lawn. Laura is sitting up in bed trying to unwind, reading a Danielle Steele novel called *Family Album*.

Despite the disorder that surrounds her, there is a sensation of calm in the house. It's the kind of feeling a long distance runner gets competing in the Boston Marathon. When she reaches the top of Heartbreak Hill, she knows the hardest part is still to come, but in her mind at least, it's all downhill.

The test of endurance began for the Grassos three days after their only child was born. The doctors told the young couple that their son had a large hole in his heart. They allowed the infant to go home until he was old enough to receive the open heart surgery that was necessary to keep him alive. Regular visits were scheduled to keep close watch on his condition. At the first appointment, the doctor took one look at Vinny and instantly noticed a yellow tinge to his skin that signified problems beyond the defective heart. Immediate tests were ordered, followed by a liver biopsy. When the results came back, Laura and Dan were told that in addition to the heart problems, their child suffered from biliary atresia. It is a rare disease that inhibits the ability of the liver to remove bile from the body. Left untreated, Vinny would die.

At five weeks of age, Vinny was wheeled into an operating room for a surgical procedure that would try to construct a bile duct out of a piece of his large intestine. If the operation was a complete success, it would mean that the newborn could expect to survive into his teenage years before he would need a liver transplant. The operation failed. Without a new liver, Vinny Grasso could not survive more than two or three years.

Before he could become a candidate for a liver transplant, however, the problem with his heart needed to be addressed. At the age of four months, he underwent open heart surgery. It was then that Dan and Laura lived through that awful moment when they had to hand over their child to a stranger wearing a mask, not knowing whether they would ever see him alive again.

Vinny proved to be a tough little kid. He came through the operation with flying colors, and not long afterward his name was placed on the organ donor list at Yale–New Haven Medical Center.

Dan and Laura carried beepers so the hospital could reach them on a moment's notice. They were told to try to stay within an hour of the hospital and to keep a bag packed. Months went by and nothing happened. Every cold and virus landed Vinny back in the hospital, and he steadily grew weaker and more jaundiced.

After a year of waiting, Laura chanced upon a woman by the name of Thelma King Thiel. Twenty-three years earlier,

Thelma King Thiel, founding executive director of the American Liver Foundation, teaches liver disease awareness and prevention to the youngest of its potential victims.

The wait over, Laura and Vinnie Grasso race to the University of Minnesota Hospital for his liver transplant.

Thelma had lost a son to biliary atresia. In those days, liver transplantation was just emerging as an option and was considered experimental surgery. In fact, her son died the same year the longest surviving liver transplant recipient received his organ.

The death of her son, Dean, was Thelma's life-altering experience. Every day for four and a half years the little boy, who bore a striking resemblance to Vinny Grasso, moved excruciatingly closer to a certain death. Thelma was a nurse, so she brought her son home and spent every waking hour caring for and comforting him, knowing that there was no hope. When it was finally over, there was an enormous void. She filled the empty space with a single desire. She wanted to find hope. She felt an overwhelming need to do something, anything, to make sure that other mothers would not go through the kind of overwhelming sense of hopelessness she endured.

She founded the country's first liver research foundation, which she named in her son's honor. Working out of her living room, she began to reach out to families all over the country who desperately needed information and support. Later she took over the reins of the newly formed American Liver Foundation as the organization's first full-time executive director. She was soon named president and CEO and nurtured the organization from infancy into a major force in the medical community.

Laura and Thelma met after Laura became involved in the Connecticut chapter of the American Liver Foundation. By that time the American Liver Foundation had become a major funder of research as well as a national clearinghouse for medical information. The organization provided a source of hope for thousands of people who suffered from any one of the more than a hundred liver diseases that make liver disease one of the top disease-related causes of death for people under the age of sixty-five. Thelma's role in providing hope was to be a national rallying force in creating prevention programs and increasing the availability of transplants. She accomplished these goals by traveling around the country organizing local chapters of the Liver Foundation in individual states. These groups initiated local prevention and education programs and helped to raise money for research that has played an important role in finding cures and helping to make transplantation a viable option.

When Thelma heard Laura's story, she recommended that the Grassos apply to be placed on the Minnesota organ donation list. Yale–New Haven Hospital performed about 6 liver transplants a year compared to the University of Minnesota, which had completed over 117 in four years.

Randy Nellis guided his car down the dark street, easing up on the accelerator as he approached a four-way intersection up ahead. He stole a glance at his sleeping daughter in the light that flashed through the car every time they passed beneath a street light. Even in her sleep, she could make him smile and shake his head, ever so slightly, from side to side. It was a gesture of continuing amazement at how deeply she had become a part of him. He couldn't explain it. He didn't even understand how she did it. All he knew was that there was this special thing that they had, a sort of secret bond that was reaffirmed every time their eyes met, every time she said "Daddy" and every time she lifted her arms up toward him in search of a hug. It was unconditional love, and it was the best thing that had ever happened to him.

He never saw the white Buick. All he heard was the crash — a sudden, deafening explosion erupting against the passenger door. Time screeched to a halt. Everything he had ever known, everything he had ever felt — his whole life, the entire universe — seemed to be suddenly, inexplicably condensed and frozen inside that single, awful millisecond when there was no up and there was no down. There was no nothing. It was like some giant superbeing touching together two high voltage cables. Sparks fly and at the moment of connection, all the lights dim, the clocks stop ticking, and everything connected to the power source ceases to exist. Then the lights come back on.

Suddenly, everything is moving too fast to comprehend. People are yelling. Sirens are blaring, red lights are flashing. Ashley is scooped up and taken away. Vicki is unconscious and trapped in the wreckage. Her head smashed against the side window, the bones in her right arm broke in the impact, and her spleen is ruptured. There's blood all over Randy. It's coming from the wounds he received on his face and head in the instant it took for him to go through the windshield and back again.

Earlier in the day, when Laura Grasso was moving into their new home, she had told her aunt about a silent prayer she had been saying every day since Vinny had been born. The prayer asked for God to look out for her son. Lately, however, she had concluded with a lighthearted afterthought asking God, "Please let us move into our new home before his liver arrives." It was a silly thing to say — more of an expression of her frustration over the lack of stability in their lives than a real wish. After all, they had been living in a bizarre limbo for two years in which everything revolved around the possibility that the phone might ring. But now that they were actually moving into the house, she felt like an obstacle had been removed and said to her aunt that she felt like something was about to happen.

Randy was sitting on the end of the emergency room gurney when the neurosurgeon approached. They had just stitched up the gash over his eye and closed up the cuts in his head. He was dazed and frantic about his family. No one would tell him what was going on, mostly because no one knew for sure. Then the words came out of the doctor's mouth in clear and simple terms. His daughter had suffered a devastating head injury. There was serious swelling of the brain. He needed to operate immediately, but the truth was, there really was no hope. Ashley was going to die. A little while later they told him that his wife was in a coma and may have suffered brain damage. They didn't know when she would regain consciousness.

Sometime later, a man by the name of Mike Olsen received a telephone call at his home in Minnesota. He was a caseworker for a non-profit organization called Lifeforce. Over the last eight years, he had become a seasoned voyager into the void. That was where he was summoned early Sunday morning on July 26, 1993. He stepped off the elevator on the fifth floor of the Ramsey Medical Center in St. Paul, Minnesota. Randy Nellis was in a small waiting room outside the Burn Unit. There had been a gas explosion in St. Paul earlier in the week and the hallway was filled with relatives and friends of the victims. When Mike Olsen walked into the waiting room, however, he was struck by the overwhelming sense of loneliness that hung in the atmosphere. The lights were turned down low and the air was thick and still. He saw the young father sitting on a cushioned chair staring straight ahead with his hands hanging limply into his lap. His cut-up face looked puffy and sore and the area around his eyes had already begun to turn black and blue.

Mike Olsen had been here before, and he had come to understand the strange and eerie ways of the place. In the void, the laws of time and space are different. A minute becomes a mammoth slice of numbing pain and space is the unfathomable distance between you and the one that is gone. Here in the void, you learn to speak slowly, not to condescend, but because you know that every word must travel through the vast emptiness and penetrate the barrier of hurt before it can be heard.

The Lifeforce caseworker knew something else about the void. It was where he found the magic. In that time and in that place where time slowed, the problems of the world became indisputably irrelevant and he could witness the essence of the human spirit. Outside the void, it's as if the spark of life within us ignites a fire that burns out of control like an oil well ablaze. It's fueled by the constant flow of energy from our egos and whipped into an inferno by gusts of wind blowing from all the other egos in our midst. It becomes so bright and so hot we have to stand far away from it, and we must shield our eyes from its intense glow. Then suddenly a fire goes out, and without warning the heat and the light and the swirling winds all stop. Then, in the calm cool air, we are able to crawl up close to where the blaze once was, and lo and behold, we see a tiny flame flickering in the empty hole. With the inferno gone, we see for the first time how beautiful the fire is, dancing innocently in the open air. When the inferno goes out, we discover that life isn't about how brightly we burn. It's about the beauty of the flickering flame.

Mike Olsen asked Randy Nellis if he wanted to think about the option of donating his daughter's organs. Randy turned and looked into his eyes as the idea sunk in. Beyond the awful sense of emptiness he felt inside, there was the overwhelming torment as he tried to put what was happening to him into some kind of rational context. One word kept screaming inside his head. Why? Why, God almighty, has this happened?

Maybe, he thought, the reason was so other children could live. It was the only thing that made any sense. Still, the decision seemed overwhelming without his wife at his side. If he could only talk to her. If he could only hold her.

Then, out of the emptiness emerged the idea that Ashley could live through the children whose lives would be saved. He told Mike Olsen he'd make the donation. He decided to keep the flame alive.

The phone rang inside the Grasso's bedroom. Laura leaned out of the bed and fumbled through stacks of boxes on the floor and came up with the handset.

"Mrs. Grasso, this is Dr. Paine from Minnesota. We think that we have a liver for your son." She jumped out of bed.

Dan, lying on his stomach, lifted his head out of the pillow and cocked one eye open. His wife mouthed the words, "It's Minnesota." Instantly, the bedroom turned into a scene like the *I Love Lucy* episode when Ricky suddenly realizes it's time to take his pregnant wife to the hospital. Still in a stupor, Dan rushed back and forth, stumbling over the boxes, trying to find clothes to throw into a bag.

Laura listened as Dr. Paine told her to get to Minnesota as fast as possible. She hung up the phone and called a special 800 number that had been given to her by a local company that had offered to donate a corporate jet for the trip. Within minutes, the two pilots were on their way to the Sikorsky Airport, a one-hour drive from the Grasso's home. Next, Laura called a relative who had made arrangements with the State Police to transport the family to the airport. The next call she made was to *Visionaries*. A film crew had been carrying beepers for two months waiting for the opportunity to share the experience with the Grasso family as part of an episode profiling the American Liver Foundation.

Five months earlier, Ari Maravel was in his office at the American Liver Foundation when the issue of the *Non-Profit Times* arrived on his desk. At least, that was the rumor. Somewhere under the stack of letters, file folders, and medical reports lay a desk. But since no one had ever actually seen it, no one was really sure. Just as no one was ever certain exactly what lay beneath the public relations director's hard-boiled facade.

He was the only son of Greek parents from the old school. After a tour in the Navy, he worked his way through Columbia University and embarked on a career in journalism.

When Ari Maravel read the brief notice about *Visionaries* in the *Non-Profit Times*, there was something about it that caught his eye. One of the sentences stated that the aim of the program was to discover "the magic that occurs when one human being helps another." At another time, in another context, the phrase would have seemed downright corny to the tough former beat reporter who cut his teeth covering crime and politics in New Jersey for various newspapers, not the least of which was the *New York Times*. Eventually, he ended up working at the institution that raised journalistic cynicism to an art form. He joined the public relations staff of CBS News, representing television's long-running magazine show, *60 Minutes*. His career at CBS ended as so many others had before and after him. Books have been written about the intense infighting within *60 Minutes* and the people who have been swallowed up by the immense egos. Ari Maravel was just another victim devoured and spit out by the system.

It seems life is always doing a strange balancing act that steadily pulls humanity back to the center whenever we drift too far off course. The media and a great deal of our energy are rightfully focused on what goes wrong when people are deprived of nurturing. Whenever a horrendous crime is committed, we almost always discover that the perpetrator is an individual who was unloved, if not abused outright, as a child.

It is interesting, however, that when we decide such situations need to be addressed, we almost always search for the answers in the failures rather than the successes. Maybe, just maybe one of the reasons we have been so unsuccessful in our quest to address so many of society's problems is that we have been looking for answers in all the wrong places.

It's only natural. In the physical world, that is what works best. If you want to know why a plane crashed, you study the wreckage. But suppose the rules were different once you entered the realm of the human psyche? What if emotion abided by a different set of laws just as liquids act differently from solids?

If you change your perspective a little bit, an interesting possibility presents itself. Using the analogy of the airplane, if you were trying to discover what made the plane fly rather than trying to determine why it crashed, how would you approach the problem? Why, you'd study it in flight, of course. You would try to discover what made it soar.

Ari Maravel, a man who spent a good part of his career poring over human wreckage, was one of the first people in America to climb aboard a flight of fantasy called *Visionaries*. He chose to see the world from a different perspective. The American Liver Foundation application was one of the first to arrive.

It stood out from the very beginning because it had two of the three elements necessary to pass the initial phase of review. First of all, there was a specific individual visionary in Thelma King Thiel, who could accompany the viewer through the episode.

The American Liver Foundation story met a second, and by far the most elusive, need. It presented an opportunity to explore one of the most profound reasons why people are drawn to philanthropic work.

Think about it. There must be a reason why two people can react so differently to adversity. In the case of Ari Maravel, we would all understand if he had become cold and bitter because of his experiences in journalism. But just the opposite occurred. He found inside of himself a reservoir of innate caring that has sustained him. Why?

Why was Thelma King Thiel, who lived through the most dreaded nightmare any parent can imagine, not destroyed by the death of her son? How did she turn the awful tragedy into a vehicle that would carry her through the rest of her life and connect her with hundreds, if not thousands, of profoundly fulfilling experiences that helped make other people's lives happier?

Visionaries could not even begin to solve such a monumental puzzle. All it could hope to do is ask the question. The issue then becomes, How do you do it? In the space of twenty-eight minutes, what can you possibly do to touch the viewer deeply enough to stimulate the process of personal inquiry? If you accept the premise that the rules for acquiring knowledge about human emotion might be different from the rules for learning about the physical universe, then you need to search for a different means of communication.

Scientists have long understood that human beings communicate on deeper and far more subtle levels than we might think. An often quoted study at a major university demonstrated that massive amounts of emotional information are transferred from one person to another in the slightest human touch. Researchers instructed employees at the university library to service two groups of randomly selected patrons identically, with one exception. In the first group, the employees touched the patron's hand when returning their library card. Outside, both groups were approached and asked to respond to a survey that rated the quality of service provided by the library. The group that had been touched rated the level of service and the professionalism of the staff far higher than the group that was treated exactly the same but had no physical contact. Most intriguing was that when the first group was asked later, most of them could not recall ever being touched by the library employee.

We all know intuitively that subtleties in facial expressions and body language as well as slight modulations in the tone of our voices can dramatically alter the power and the very meaning of the words that we speak. It is these non-verbal means of communication that constitute the language of emotion.

That is why documentary television has such a difficult time connecting with viewers. In the process of collecting and then disseminating information, it is easy to lose sight of the fact that saying the words is only a small part of delivering the message.

There are only two methods of telling the whole story on issues that relate to the human condition. The first is through drama. Since the ancient Greeks, actors on stage have worked to master the art of pretending to possess the emotion their characters would feel in real life. The second way is to witness the actual events that create the emotions you wish to explore.

This was the creative challenge that was presented by the first program selected for inclusion in *Visionaries*. How can the viewer understand the depth of emotion that is experienced by someone like Thelma King Thiel that ultimately puts them on the road to a life dedicated to serving other people? This component of the show was particularly important because the service she delivered on a daily basis fell into the area of education and disease prevention. Therefore, the third component necessary for a group to be selected, the opportunity to see the direct delivery of services, did not have the emotional impact some of the other *Visionaries* episodes would ultimately demonstrate.

The idea was to follow a family that was going through the same kind of experience that Thelma King Thiel had endured over two decades earlier. This process would allow the viewer to see and feel the depth of emotion a parent experiences in a moment of crisis. At the same time, it would demonstrate a critical difference between Thelma's story and the experience of a parent of a child with a similar condition today. Today, the parent has hope. A big reason there is hope today is because of visionaries like Thelma King Thiel, who dedicated their lives to raise the resources for the research that has led to new and innovative treatments like transplantation.

Before the creative challenge of finding a way for the viewer to share the kind of life-altering experience that Thelma endured, there was a much more practical problem that needed to be solved: funding.

The traditional method followed by almost everyone who has ever produced a documentary series for public television is to create a concept and then apply for funding. The way the system is supposed to work is that foundations and corporations provide the money to produce the program, and in exchange for their support they receive an on-screen acknowledgment at the end of the broadcast.

In reality, however, this route is reserved almost exclusively for a small, select group of producers with firmly established contacts within the public broadcasting community.

New ideas that break new ground are required to come up with new sources of funding. That's not a bad system, but rather an appropriate gauntlet that requires an idea to prove its worth in the competitive marketplace.

Visionaries needed to prove itself in the marketplace more than most programs because it was not genre specific. It sought to break new ground in both subject matter and approach to the medium. The only way to accomplish that goal was simply to go out and do it; then the proof would be in the product. Up until a show is finished, the rest is all blue smoke and mirrors. But once an episode is in the can, it's either good or it isn't. It either touches you or it doesn't.

An essential component of the *Visionaries* concept was the idea that there existed a whole reservoir of potential funding that could be tapped by using a slight variation of the established method of raising funds for public television. The usual and most logical approach is for the producer of a particular program to identify the funders that would most benefit from association with the program. Obviously, that is why day care centers sponsor children's programing and why building supply companies pay to have a tag placed at the end of shows about home improvement. The problem, of course, is that this pool of funds is extremely limited, and those groups most interested in supporting public television have already been tapped many times over and have already established relationships with particular programs and producers.

A unique resource to find financial support existed within the organizations that were chosen to be profiled. Almost every group had a volunteer or staff person whose primary job was to seek out and find the foundations and corporations that cared about their work.

The plan, therefore, was to select a group of finalists without regard to their access to funding resources and then involve them in the process of seeking sponsors by contacting companies, foundations, and even individuals who understood the need to increase public awareness of that particular issue.

In the beginning, this approach presented a couple of problems. First of all, *Visionaries* was only an idea. There was no

commitment from public broadcasting to air the program, and
although other outlets like the Discovery Channel, Lifetime,
and other cable channels were being actively pursued, there
was nothing close to a guarantee that the program would ever
be seen on television.

This meant that if *Visionaries* was going to attract a sponsor
for individual episodes, it would have to find a way of doing it
without being able to offer the all-important sponsorship tags
as a way to reward the donor. Without the sponsorship tag,
the ability to raise the kind of money that is usually spent on a
typical PBS program was dramatically diminished.

Most people in the broadcast television industry would assume that the cost of a half-hour documentary-style program
would be about $250,000. Many, if not most, spend much
more. For example, *The Quiet Revolution,* a series of six half-
hour programs with a theme similar to *Visionaries* and shot in
similar locations and produced during the same period of time,
cost $350,000 per episode.

There was simply no way on earth that the relatively
small individual supporters could come up with this kind of
money. Moreover, it would be something of an ethical absur-
dity to approach a foundation to support a documentary on
the Human Service Alliance with a contribution of $350,000
when the total annual budget of the organization was only
$65,000.

The reality of the situation required that a different standard be used. Many non-profit organizations around the country use locally produced videos to get their message out to
the public. These "industrials" or "presentation videos" have
become an essential tool in the development of an organization. Entire fundraising, volunteer recruitment, and public
education campaigns are built around a single video.

A non-profit organization will pay a local company using
non-broadcast-quality equipment anywhere from $35,000 to
$60,000 to produce a fifteen- to thirty-minute video. Even
though each episode of *Visionaries* was going to be shot and
edited on the far more expensive broadcast quality equipment,
airing on television was not assured. Therefore, if the show

never ended up on the air, all the underwriter would be left with is a high quality presentation video.

Making this problem even more acute is the fact that the Public Broadcasting System has instituted regulations that attempt to discourage producers from seeking funding on an episode-by-episode basis. These rules take the form of forbidding the placement of a different sponsorship tag at the end of each individual episode. Whatever tag appears at the end of one program must appear on all episodes. Therefore, even if the goal of getting the show on the air was achieved, the individual donor could not be given a sponsorship tag.

The bottom line was that if *Visionaries* was going to go out and prove that high quality, emotion-evoking, and positive programing could be produced, it was going to have to do it on a budget that was 80 percent below the industry standard.

In the nearly two years the Grasso family had been waiting for the organ that could save their child's life, they had imagined what it would be like when the call came. In these dreams, there would be a neatly packed bag filled with the clothes and toiletries that they would scoop up on the way to the waiting police cruiser. When the call actually came, all their clothes were still in unmarked cardboard boxes stacked up in the garage. They ran down the front steps, across the freshly seeded lawn, and jumped into the police cruiser with only the clothes on their backs.

Meanwhile, an equally unprepared film crew arrived at a small airport in the town of Norwood, Massachusetts, ten miles south of Boston. There was only a producer and a cameraman, and whatever equipment they could carry on their backs. The airplane that would take them to Connecticut was owned by Paul Schneiders, a successful attorney and private pilot. Months earlier, he and his son, Bobby, also a pilot, had volunteered to carry a beeper and make the flight from Norwood to Bridgeport, Connecticut, at their own expense. They were the first of dozens of volunteers who would make up for the lack of funding.

What funding that did exist for the program came from the most unlikely of sources. Prescription drug companies, medical foundations, and a half dozen major corporations all turned down requests to support the program. Finally, two individuals who had a personal interest in increasing public awareness about liver disease came forward to share the $40,000 cost of the program. The first was country and western star Naomi Judd, who suffers from chronic hepatitis, a liver disease. The second donor was Marty Richards, the Broadway producer of hits like *Will Rogers Follies*. His wife died of liver disease.

As the Connecticut State Police cruiser sped through the night at speeds approaching a hundred miles an hour, the trooper kept the siren wailing and the blue lights flashing, making the normally hour-long drive in a little over twenty minutes. Dan was in the front seat and Laura sat in the back, cradling her son in her lap.

Overhead, Paul Schneiders and his son, Bobby, were in the cockpit of the four-seater, peering through the darkness, trying to find the small, unmanned airport. Scanning through the radio dial, they made contact with the pilot of the corporate jet who reported that the family was now on board and ready to leave. The runway lights suddenly flashed on and Paul Schneiders swung around and dropped immediately into a landing pattern.

On the ground, the four-seater taxied up to the jet and the camera crew ran from one plane to the other, pausing only long enough to get a quick shot of the jet. Inside, Dan and Laura were wearing nervous smiles as the twin engines wound up to take-off speed as the plane catapulted down the runway. On the wall of the cabin was a digital speedometer that let the passengers know the cruising speed. The plane leveled off at 660 miles per hour.

Dan and Laura, their voices cracking with emotion, talked

about the donor family. They did not know who they were and would not learn their identity for over a year, but they recognized what they had done was an act of giving that was almost beyond human comprehension.

When the plane touched down, a taxi was waiting on the tarmac to ferry them across the city to the University of Minnesota Medical Center. Not far away at the Ramsey Medical Center, Randy Nellis was standing beside his wife, who was now out of surgery. Her fractured right arm was in a cast and a white bandage covered her severe head injury. She would remain unconscious until the day of her daughter's funeral, six days after the accident.

At about the same time, a medical team was arriving at the hospital from the University of Minnesota. They were the harvest team. They removed Ashley's liver and placed it in a red and white plastic beach cooler with the words "Human Organ" printed on the cover. While Ashley was still connected to a breathing machine, her heart, lungs and kidney were also removed and rushed to other recipients.

Outside the operating room at the University of Minnesota, Dr. William Paine approached the Grasso family huddled together in the corner of the large pre-op room. Tears were now flowing down Laura's face, and she dabbed at her eyes with a crumpled-up tissue. Dan, a strong, quiet man, sucked in his chest, gritted his teeth, and fought back the wave of emotion. He bowed his head and hid his eyes from the video camera that was recording the scene. If he had looked up he would have seen that the *Visionaries* crew were crying as well.

Then the moment finally arrived. The parents stood. The son's fate and the course of their lives hung in the balance. Laura passed Vinny into the hands of the nurse who would take him into the operating room. It was at that instant — in the moment of separation — that they stepped into the void with Vicki and Randy Nellis. Nothing would ever be the same again.

— ✥ —

Today, Laura and Dan Grasso say that Vinny is as healthy as a horse. Their dreams have came true.

Randy Nellis and his wife, Vicki, have a new child, born a year after the accident. But the memory of Ashley is always with them, as is a lingering sense of loss that will never go away.

So what is the moral of the story? If there is a lesson to be learned, it will be discovered in the void. It is out of this place that grew the American Liver Foundation and hundreds, if not thousands, of organizations founded, staffed, and supported by the donations of people who have been there. Something magical happens when all the frivolous inventions of our egos are stripped away and we are made to see what really matters. That's not corny. The stories don't have neat happy endings. In fact, most of the time, as Randy and Vicki Nellis will attest, it's a horrible lesson to learn. But when you remove all of the emotion, stop keeping score, forget about winners and losers, eliminate petty judgments and hopeless attempts to have it all come out sweet and pretty, one indisputable truth remains: When Randy Nellis stood alone in the vast expanse of emptiness, he had a choice. He could fill the vacuum with hate and bitterness, or he could choose another course. When the most important thing in Vicki and Randy Nellis's life was gone, when they had nothing, they chose to do something extraordinary. They chose to give.

CHAPTER SEVEN

The Heart
Has Its Reasons

*The more you examine the
common traits of today's
visionaries, the more you begin
to see that a key component of
their personalities is a belief in
the power of human emotion.*

A FEW HUNDRED YEARS AGO, most men, women, and children in the world believed, with absolute certainty, that the earth was flat. The idea that it might be otherwise required a change in perspective that contradicted virtually every bit of available physical evidence. More amazing still, believing the world was round required people to accept the existence of a mysterious unseen force called gravity.

Today, humankind's great explorers are trying to find their way to another new world. These are people like the visionaries who are looking for discoveries about life within the relationships between people. Unlike Newton and Galileo, these great thinkers are not studying the physical universe; they are entering the realm of emotional reality.

The visionaries of old needed to move beyond the perspective afforded them by their human senses. After all, the world looked flat and you could not hear the planet turning on its axis just as you could not smell or touch gravity. It requires no greater leap of logic to believe that there is another whole world worthy of exploration within the universe of human emotion: the place where feelings dwell.

We like to think of ourselves as great rational beings who

have built a society on reliable concepts founded in science and logic. How absurd. Select any hour of any day in any person's life and objectively analyze what that person did and why he or she did it. Every conscious choice we make is an emotional decision. Why does a person get up and go to work? He *enjoys* his job; she *needs* the money; he *wants* a promotion; she's *loyal* to her co-workers; he's *afraid* of getting fired. In every instance, the underlying motivation is an emotional feeling. It doesn't matter whether it's joy, loyalty, fear, or desire; we do what we do because of what we feel.

Even though all of humanity revolves around emotion, we have yet to evolve beyond the limitation of our primitive egos that convince us that we created the world through increasingly brilliant strokes of logic.

This twisted view of who we are and why we do the things we do is accomplished in part by the perception that one type of thought is superior to another. Since early childhood, we are taught that analytical thoughts are more substantive than feelings of love or caring. We are even made to believe that emotions are not thoughts at all, but some primitive sensations that don't even originate in the brain but in the heart.

This gigantic cultural bias is so powerful that if anyone ever did get a federal grant to study human kindness, that person would be hauled before a congressional committee and vilified for wasting taxpayers' money. On the other hand, dropping a few million dollars to study serial killers makes a lot of sense because the number of people being killed by mass murderers is rapidly approaching the number of people who get struck by lightning every year.

The question then becomes, Where does this feeling that feelings aren't important come from? As bizarre as it may seem, the answer is purely logical. Over the last 150 years, scientists have slowly come to understand that the human brain is not a single organ, but two separate spheres with remarkably different functions. Even before modern medicine had the means to explore inside the brain it was known that the left half of the brain controls language. This was proven by comparing individuals who had sustained similar injuries to different hemispheres of the brain. Those with the left-side injuries lost the ability to use language while those with an injury to the right side did not.

In the last twenty years, remarkable new information has emerged from work done by Dr. Roger W. Sperry and his associates at the California Institute of Technology. Part of their research involved sophisticated tests performed on a group of people who had previously undergone a radical surgical procedure. This operation severed their *corpus callosum*, which is the collection of nerve endings that connects one half of the brain to the other. This operation succeeded in ending the life-threatening epileptic seizures these patients suffered, apparently caused by the interaction of the two hemispheres. After a period of recovery, the patients appeared to return to normal without the seizures and suffered no obvious disabilities in motor skills, cognitive function, or language ability even though the two halves of their brains now operated independently.

These patients, who became known as the *commissurotomy*, or "split-brain," patients, presented a unique opportunity for study. Dr. Sperry and his students devised a series of ingenious tests to determine what role the two hemispheres of the brain played.

The amazing conclusion of this research revealed that each half of the brain literally sees the world differently. The left, language-oriented hemisphere is analytical, synthesizing and storing information using cold concrete symbols to represent ideas. The right brain, on the other hand, sorts the same data differently. It processes the thoughts into feelings that categorize the information according to emotional sensations. When a person looks at a tree, the physical symbol of a tree is imprinted on the left half of the brain like a typewriter hammering out the tree key. The right hemisphere sees the same tree and is awed by its beauty, bored by its plainness, or moved by the allure of its majestic limbs to climb up into a comfortable perch. The important point is to understand that Dr. Sperry's research clearly demonstrated a dominance of human thought by the left, analytical portion of the brain.

Dr. Betty Edwards of California State University has taken Dr. Sperry's research and produced a remarkable demonstration of the practical ramifications of left-brain domination. In her book *Drawing on the Right Side of the Brain,* she systematically illustrates how we lose the ability to accomplish specific creative tasks as we grow out of childhood. As our language skills increase and the left half of the brain grows more dominant, there is often a corresponding decrease in our ability to tap into the awesome power of the right brain.

Her book, which has sold well over a million copies in eight languages, brilliantly leads the reader through a series of simple exercises that shut off the left brain and turn on the right. The result is that, almost overnight, tens of thousands of people who thought they had no artistic talent have learned to draw. They have accomplished this without any art instruction. She has proven that by simply opening up the inherent skills locked away in the right brain, almost anyone can produce a work of art.

What makes this research and its practical application so important is that it gives insight into the mental process that is silently at work creating the belief that our feelings are less important than our analytical thoughts.

The signals emanating from the creative right brain into the *corpus callosum* are feelings. The left brain achieves dominance by negating the value of these messages with whatever analytical weapons it has at its disposal. This is the reason we tend to think that emotional subject matter is less relevant than intellectual thoughts. The irony, of course, is that science, the place where the left brain goes for self-worship, now has been caught in its own web, by proving the importance of its archrival through a process of analytical thought.

As Betty Edwards states in her book, "The tests provide surprising new evidence that each hemisphere, in a sense, perceives its own reality — or perhaps better stated, perceives reality in its own way. The verbal half of the brain — the left half dominates — most of the time . . . the right, non-speaking half of the brain also experiences, responds with feelings, and processes information on its own."

The more you examine the common traits of today's visionaries, the more you begin to see that a key component of their personalities is a belief in the power of human emotion. Like Betty Edwards's aspiring artists, they have learned the skill of turning off the nagging naysayer that keeps trying to invalidate what they feel. The result is they "perceive reality in their own way."

What seems to happen to people like Gladys Sylvestre and the volunteers at the Human Service Alliance is that once they begin to allow their right brain to dominate, or at least gain parity, the door is open for remarkable things to happen. Scientists now know that intuition, original ideas, and spontaneous insight originate in the same hemisphere as emotion. Most people, however, can't hear these messages because their analytical minds are making too much noise or are busy convincing them that these "silly feelings" are invalid.

Suppose it is possible that we have been unable to solve some of our most vexing problems because the answers are concealed from us.

In categorizing Dr. Sperry's research at Cal Tech, Dr. Edwards states in her book, "As a result of these extraordinary findings over the past fifteen years, we now know that despite our normal feelings we are one person — a single being — our brains are double, each half with its own way of knowing, its own way of perceiving reality. . . . Furthermore it may be that each hemisphere has a way of keeping knowledge from the other hemisphere. It may be, as the saying goes, that the right hand truly doesn't know what the left hand is doing."

In Bogota, Colombia, ten thousand children wander the cruel, unforgiving streets scraping and clawing their way through every day. Where did they come from? Why are they here? Some were brought here from the countryside by their parents, who were lured to the city by the enticing aroma of rising expectations. Other children, for one reason or another, found themselves alone and simply followed the road. All roads eventually lead to the city. Others, still, were driven from their homes by abuse so horrendous that sleeping in a cardboard box in an alley where young killers prowl seemed safer than returning home.

Fernando was seven years old when he stepped onto the road. Those days are blurry now, but he remembers being told that his mother and father drowned crossing a river in the town where he was born. To this day he doesn't know the details. All he remembers is being alone and following the road. He walked for days on end scrounging for food. Finally, he arrived in the city. He was just one more kid without a home struggling to live off the refuse of the people he saw driving past in their cars. He'd hold out his hand and beg when they came to a stop at the intersections in the center of the crowded city. Most would wave him away, spitting out the word that carried with it all the incrimination of a so-ciety that looked upon street children as rodents worthy of extermination.

On the day he arrived in the city, he became a *gambino*. The word means disposable. But it is not just a slur; to many it is a literal description of the value of the children who live off of the streets. Vigilante gangs of otherwise respectable citizens wander the alleys at night exterminating six- and seven-year-old boys sleeping in the trash. In broad daylight, the fire department cruises about looking for street children to assault with their high pressure hoses. And as any kid on the street will tell you, getting arrested by the wrong police officer is the equivalent of a death sentence.

Despite the ever-present danger, Fernando found the city to have a strange allure that in some indefinable way helped to distract him from the sense of emptiness that he felt at the loss of his parents. He was from the countryside, and the sights and sounds of the city filled him with amazement. The fast, shiny cars, the tall, brightly lit buildings, and the huge crowds of hurrying people struck him with a sense of wonder. It seemed at first like a place overflowing with wealth and abundance.

In his first days in the city, he survived by scrounging through trash cans behind the fancy restaurants that lined the downtown streets. There, in the back alleys, he met other young boys — some of whom took it upon themselves to teach him the ropes. Fernando become a master observer, watching and listening closely to the ways of the street. There was a simple but absolute set of rules, and he learned them quickly. The first rule was to survive. Do whatever you have to do to live. The second rule was that the only way to stay alive was to live by your instincts.

The reality of that fact became viciously real not long after he arrived in Bogota. It had been a good day. His belly was full and in one of the pockets of his filthy torn pants was enough money to get through another day. He and his friends had staked out an area behind an apartment complex. There was a retaining wall that sheltered them from the wind and plenty of newspapers they could sleep beneath. Fernando had dozed off an hour or two before dawn. He was sleeping on his back and his head was turned to the side and tilted back, exposing his neck in the glow of a nearby street light.

Another boy, hungry and desperate, had been sitting in the shadows for hours waiting for his chance. His belly ached and the only thing that kept him alert was the memory of Fernando stuffing the wad of cash in his pants pocket earlier in the night.

In a crouch, he slowly crept across the sea of bodies, carefully placing a pointed toe in between a head and arm here, a shoulder and leg there. As he closed in, he silently drew a rusty steak knife tucked in his pants and circled around so that his shadow would not cross Fernando's face. For a moment, he paused, biting his lower lip and drawing a slow, deep breath through his nose. He swallowed hard and leaned back on his haunches, ready to make the plunge. Fernando stirred. The boy reacted instantly, lunging for his throat. The dull edge of the blade found Fernando's neck and began scraping a path through the skin toward his jugular. Fernando bolted upright, his arms instinctively jerking toward the pain. Instantly, he found a wrist in his vice-like grip and struggled to tear the knife away from his neck. He let out the scream his assailant was hoping to avoid by slitting his throat and the layer of bodies around him sprung alert. As his friends struggled to their senses, Fernando twisted the knife to the side and hit the other boy with a head butt to the bridge of his nose. Still gripping the knife-wielding fist with both hands, he twisted the wrist while bending it backward. With one solid thrust of his body, he jammed the serrated edge into the boy's stomach just below the rib cage. There was an awful sucking sound as the blade traveled up and punctured the eleven-year-old boy's lung. Fernando let go and his assailant stumbled backward, still holding onto the knife. He took two steps, then his legs weakened and buckled, dropping him to his knees. Blood came out of his mouth in coughs; then he fell forward onto the knife.

Father Xavier had been working in Bogota for years, and like the rest of the population, he managed to go about his life without allowing himself to feel any connection with the children on the street. It was only over time that he learned to put aside the part of him that kept sending out signals to mitigate the emotions he felt whenever he saw a child curled up in a doorway. When he found himself pondering the plight of street children, instantly thoughts would arrive to offset his concern. He'd think, "Well, kids are resilient, they'll do okay," or "Hey, if they didn't want to be on the street they would go out and get a job." Or worse still, "They're different from me; they don't know any better."

Father Xavier had grown up in Italy during World War II, and he had seen childhood friends forced out onto the street by the horrors of war. These strong emotional images lingered and, as much as his analytical mind tried to explain them away, they kept re-emerging. Every time they did, they looked more and more like Colombian street children. He be-

Father Xavier embraces the former street children living at La Florida, a safe and loving enclave of hope.

Father Xavier touches the lives of every person he meets, old and young, living on the streets of Bogota, Colombia.

gan to feel a need to connect with these feelings in order to understand their meaning.

He went about the job slowly, like a research project. The first step was to try to figure out what made the kids tick. Why were they on the street and what forces were at work that kept them from finding a way to break away and move into the normal flow of society? In the beginning, simply getting close to the children was extremely difficult. Authority figures of every kind were viewed as dangerous enemies to be avoided at all cost. Father Xavier needed to eliminate the fear of the unknown, not just in the minds of the children, but on his part as well. To accomplish this, he simply began to venture out into the streets at night. He wandered through the dark alleys where the gambinos bought and sold drugs, and he sat with them as they sniffed glue inside abandoned buildings or under the cover of an unlit doorway.

He realized from the very beginning that his role could not be judgmental. He knew, of course, that what the children were doing was not only illegal, but potentially deadly. He also understood, however, that if he was ever going to comprehend their lives, he would have to share their experiences without the conflict created by the act of inflicting his own code of conduct on people who were living by a totally different set of laws. Through this process of silently witnessing the experiences of the children, he slowly began to feel an ever-deepening connection with the forces that propelled them through each day teetering on the very edge of survival.

It was as if a door had opened into a whole new world. Inside this place, the hues and texture of life were different. Just as the color brown is not inherently better or worse than green, life on the streets seemed less and less to be about good and bad as it was simply different. Once you made the transition and passed through the portal from one world to the other, your perspective changed to the extent that you no longer perceived the children's lives to be wholly devoid of happiness and joy. You began to see that their wants and needs were actually identical to the desires of everyone else.

The difference was in the means available to them to fulfill the fundamental physical and emotional needs every person has.

The difficulty that society has in dealing with situations like street children in the Third World, or the homeless in America, or even juvenile delinquency and crime in general, is that we try to find solutions by judging the problems from our perspective rather than theirs. We constantly say to ourselves, whether we like to admit it or not, "If I was in their position, I'd just do this or I'd do that." The problem, of course, is that if you were in their position, you wouldn't be in their position.

Father Xavier soon discovered that the gambinos' behavior was really a normal reaction to the most basic of human needs that fell into a surprisingly simple and predictable pattern. At the lowest gut level was the raw biological quest for survival. A child, like any human organism, needs food, water, and protection from the elements and from predators. Thousands of children all over the world are living at this level. Moral issues boil down to choices between life and death. Children hover near outdoor cafes waiting to pounce on unguarded table scraps because the choice is, do I steal that piece of bread or do I die? While that single morsel of food may not be the difference between living and starving to death, the human body sends powerful signals. What these children know instinctively is that if they don't eat something soon, they will become so weakened from hunger that they won't be able to physically protect themselves from predators in the night.

On the streets of Bogota, Father Xavier made a more important discovery than Darwin's explanation for the behavior of Colombia's street children. He walked the streets night after night, and slowly the children began to take him into their confidence. He began taking groups of kids out of the city on day trips where he would have a chance to talk to them, one on one, in a more secure setting than was possible on the streets. In one unguarded conversation after another, there emerged another simple but profound truth. The emotional needs of the children were no less powerful than the need for food and water. Each and every gambino seemed to be propelled through an agonizing array of crimes and violent acts by a set of twin engines. One was powered by the body's need to survive and the other by the soul.

As the years went by for Fernando, the killing became easier and easier. He became emboldened by the power and the prestige that his mastery of the street brought to him. Respect of his peers seemed an adequate substitute for love and affection.

Then, one day, something happened. It's hard to pinpoint the reasons why; it was just the way of the street. Fernando was milling around with his friends. He was older and more powerful than ever before. His pockets were full again, and as his best friend approached, there was the kind of swagger in his step that comes only to those who have mastered the illusion of self-confidence. Fernando took notice and nodded his head approvingly as if to say, "Yeah, you're cool, but not quite cool enough."

The friend was in a playful mood. He took a good-natured jab toward Fernando's face and then danced around on his tiptoes with his fists at the ready. Fernando dodged the blow easily and dismissed his friend with a wave of the hand. They'd been playing this game since they were both pups competing for table scraps. Now, however, Fernando was the top dog and deserved to be treated with respect.

Maybe the friend thought that their relationship was an exception to the rules. After all, they had been together before there were any rules. Whatever the reason, he came back again, dancing on his toes, shadow boxing annoyingly close to Fernando's face. The others began to gather around, circling the two and making sounds to egg them on. Not once, but twice, Fernando tried to exert his authority magnanimously, but each time the friend came back for more. On the third try, he plunged forward and caught Fernando in a headlock. They struggled, both trying to keep a humorous edge on the encounter but the rules of engagement left no room to maneuver. Every action required a stronger reaction. Anything less would be a sign of weakness. In the scuffle, the friend

found a way to break off the physical encounter with a show
of bravado. He reached into Fernando's pocket and extracted
a few crumpled up bills.

They separated. The friend held up the notes as a sign
of triumph. Fernando, seething now at the act of defiance,
stretched his hand toward his friend and angrily motioned
with a pull of his fingers for him to turn over the money. Fernando's friend laughed. It was a terrible mistake. The smile
melted from his face and the laughter coming from the crowd
petered out ominously. Fernando dropped his hand, turned his
head to the side, and shot a sidelong glance across the ten feet
that separated them.

It had already gone too far, and both of them seemed to
know that there was no turning back. The friend lifted the
bills to Fernando and told him if he wanted his money back,
he'd have to come get it. Fernando did . . . first with his fists.
The fifteen-year-old boys pummeled each other into bloody
pulps with a huge crowd now surrounding them, screaming for
an honorable conclusion.

No one knows where the knives came from. They were just
tossed into the fray. The friend was the first to pick up his
weapon, but it did not matter; they both knew there was no
turning back. Fernando dodged a roundhouse slash toward his
face and then plunged toward his friend's chest, but missed.
On the counterthrust, the friend drew the first blood, opening a slice in Fernando's arm. In defense, Fernando moved
in close to counteract the wide, sweeping slashes. Shoulder
to shoulder, he found his opening, and in a single, devastating thrust, rammed the seven-inch blade into his friend's
stomach until he felt the hilt touch flesh. Then he twisted
it with a grunt. The crowd gasped in disbelief. The injured
boy's eyes went wide and locked on Fernando's face as the
sudden realization of what had happened washed over both
of them.

The boy staggered, his mouth agape, sucking in gasps of air.
Fernando let go of the knife and wrapped his arms around his
friend to ease him to the ground. Fernando looked down at
the knife sticking out of his friend's belly and then up into his

glazed-over eyes. He saw a word forming in his mouth as the boy forced his mouth closed. "Why?"

The sound rode out on his last wisp of breath. Before Fernando could answer, his best friend was dead.

— —

Once Father Xavier saw the clear needs of the children, he acted. The first step was to establish a program within the city that would help to relieve the all-consuming drive to survive. He built what is called a Patio. It was a drop-in center. Here a child could come in off the streets for a hot meal and a shower. The rules were simple and non-judgmental. The staff would ask no questions. You didn't have to give your name. It didn't matter if the police were hunting for you. The only thing that mattered was that you left all drugs and weapons outside.

As word spread throughout the city, hundreds of children swarmed to the shelter, lured by the offer of meals they didn't have to steal or fight for to obtain. One of those boys was Fernando.

Inside the Patio, Father Xavier watched and tried to view the world through the eyes of the hundreds of children, like Fernando who wandered in and then back out again. He came to realize that a powerful tug of war was going on inside of the gambinos. The food and the warmth and security of the Patio were a strong lure to the children, but there was something equally strong that pulled them back out onto the streets. It took a while, but he came to understand that the street provided a sustenance for the children's psyche that fulfilled them as much as the hot stew served in the shelter.

Fernando had already learned the skills needed to survive. The mastery of the streets filled him with a strong sense of competence and self-worth that fed his young ego like a tonic. To make it through each day, he was forced to form an alliance with other children, and they organized themselves into groups for protection. The individual gangs took on the role of the family, providing nurture and comfort to members who demonstrated unswerving loyalty. Still, there was a lingering emptiness in all the children that seemed to come from an un-conscious realization that something was missing deeper inside of them than they could understand. They filled the cavern with the warm, euphoric glow provided by drugs.

Father Xavier began to send teams of youth workers out into the street at night to reach out to the children and to spread the word about the safe havens he was now building in more and more neighborhoods. Ever so slowly, a phenom-enon began to occur. It began with just one youngster, then another, and soon it became clear that a growing number of kids wanted to find a way to permanently leave the streets behind. At first, it was children who had originally made a conscious decision to enter the streets in the first place. They had been running from abusive homes or were lured away by the strong camaraderie they discovered inside the gang cul-ture. These children now were ready to make another choice. This one was to find a way to leave the streets and enter the mainstream of society. Certainly they had had plenty of oppor-tunity to see that there was a whole other world that they had been excluded from because of the prejudice of people who considered them little more than rodents worthy of extermi-nation. But in the process of wandering throughout the city, they had seen how the rest of the world lived. It was there in plain view in the windows of the fancy shops and in fancy cars driving past them.

Father Xavier committed himself to providing an escape route for those children who had made a personal decision to leave the streets. He opened a new program called Bosco-nia, named after the founder of the Salesian missionary order, Don Bosco. Bosconia was a residential facility where the chil-dren could go to live once they decided that they wanted to leave the streets behind. This was not a casual decision, and as much as it may seem so from the perspective of someone on the outside looking in, it was anything but an easy deci-sion. At work here were the same kinds of powerful forces that keep young people in the inner cities of America held captive to street gangs. It is their only source for all the emotional nu-trients they need to survive. It is where they get their love and affection, it is where they get their self-esteem, and it is the place where their egos are moored.

Nonetheless, every morning when dawn breaks, the streets are littered with the dead bodies of children who did not make it through the night. The longer a gambino lived on the street, the more he came to realize that it was just a matter of time before it would eat him alive.

If Father Xavier had learned anything in the years it took him to build five Patios throughout the city and to institute the Bosconia program, it was that the most essential ingredient in getting a kid off of the street was in fulfilling his emotional needs. It was all about love and affection.

Every aspect of the residential program was built to ensure that the child who came into the program was treated as an individual who the staff cared about as a person. Rules were kept simple, but absolute. No drugs, no violence, and everyone had an important role to play. It was during the process of building new lives in Bosconia that Father Xavier came to a startling realization. The kids that were emerging out of the Patios and into the residential program seemed to have a remarkable quality in common. They were all winners. Although they lived in an institution, they attended public schools. In the classroom, a surprising number excelled even though they had been deprived of much of the early formal education their classmates had benefited from. When they finished school and went out into the work force, many of them did better than their counterparts who had grown up in traditional family settings.

The strange paradox that emerged out of Bosconia was the realization that the children who Colombia's society had branded with the label of the disposables were actually exactly the opposite. What seemed to be happening was that the Darwinian existence on the street seemed to be creating a crop of children who acquired astounding survival skills. Those who managed to live long enough to find their way into the Patio and then demonstrate the commitment necessary to earn entrance to Bosconia were the smartest, most cunning kids in the country. On the street, kids like Fernando learned skills like multiple option thinking, group dynamics, and crisis management.

The realization that he had stumbled across a group of children who had the potential to accomplish much more than anyone had anticipated created new challenges. Where in the beginning their only hope was to save the lives of children teetering on the edge of oblivion, new hope and new goals emerged out of the potential demonstrated by the gambinos who chose to leave the streets and make Bosconia their home.

Soon, an entirely new program was conceived that represented a third tier in Father Xavier's escape route from the streets. It is called La Florida and was built on a cow pasture outside the city, not far from the international airport. Here, bright and airy dormitories were built around a huge, tiled courtyard in the center of which rose a tower with the likeness of Don Bosco painted on the side.

Dawn comes slowly to the moist, fertile valley where La Florida sits like a concrete oasis in a pastureland of dozing cows. Rugged mountains on the easterly horizon hold back the rays of sunshine until the sky overhead is already illuminated in cool steely blue light. A thick, dank blanket of fog is levitating just above the ground when reveille blows through megaphones bolted to a light pole. The rousing call echoes against the geometric brick walls of the twelve dormitories that each house fourteen boys.

Before the second verse is finished, the patter of running feet fills the courtyard and the boys assemble in neat rows holding brooms in their hands. There are no adults in sight. In the front of the assembly is a group of older boys directing their charges into line.

La Florida is the ultimate experiment in the power of personal choice. Once Father Xavier began to see the world through the eyes of the children who had already learned lessons and survived trials most adults could never endure, he had a clear view of what would work and what would not.

The idea was simply this. In the Patios and later in Bosconia, take every opportunity to feed the children emotionally.

At least once every day, single out every child and connect with him on an emotional level. Listen when the children speak, hear what they say. And respond to their needs as best as you can. This emotional contact will sustain them and stimulate growth. By giving love in this way, you must trust in the natural process of emotional growth and believe that the answer to each child's problems is not in you, but in them.

La Florida is the ultimate expression of that process. It is an institution designed to promote emotional growth through validating the decision each child makes on his own behalf. Within each dormitory, the children elect their own house father. They pick the leader who most fulfills their needs. This representative serves on a legislative body that creates the rules and provides a forum for debating issues. The daily operation of La Florida is overseen by a mayor who is elected by the children. This form of self-government has resulted in the creation of a La Florida bank that prints its own currency. The children earn this money for the work they perform before and after school. They use it to purchase clothes and other products at the La Florida stores created and operated by other children.

After assembly in the morning, each child attends classes that will earn him a high school diploma. Some will be trained in computers, architectural design, and mechanical drawing. Others opt to be trained in the carpentry, pottery, or metal fabrication shop. All of the children participate in music programs, and the school has its own orchestra, which performs around the country.

The Colombian government and, in fact, most institutions in the world, approach the problem from a different perspective. When they analyze the situation, they institute solutions founded on non-emotional, so-called objective criteria. When the right half of the brain does not participate in the process of assessing the needs of children and developing programs, the result is solutions that take on all of the characteristics of left-brain thinking. The government of Colombia looks at street children and sees the problem as a lack of structure, poor dis-

cipline, and a breakdown of authority. Its solution: hit the key
that punches out the ultimate symbol for structure, discipline,
and authority: jail.

Father Xavier, through a process of shared experience that
allowed him to feel what was going on inside the children's
minds, came to realize that the answer required a meeting of
the minds. Looking at the situation holistically, it seemed that
the reason the children acted out in often violent ways was
that they had been deprived of the essential emotional nu-
trients of love and affection. This emotional malnourishment
produced symptoms like drug abuse, violent aggression, and
shockingly low self-esteem. Treating the illness by forcing the
children to stop the behavior would be like treating famine
by ordering starving children to suck in their stomachs and to
stop foraging for food. You would eliminate the symptoms but
in both cases the patient dies.

In La Florida, the phenomenon of remarkable accomplishment first witnessed in Bosconia accelerated. Over the years,
ten thousand children, the equivalent of the entire population
of street children in Bogota, have successfully completed the
program; 90 percent have received their high school diplomas.
Not only have thousands of children been transformed from
criminals to craftsmen; over half of the members of the Bogota
Symphony Orchestra are graduates of La Florida. Throughout
the city, scores of tradesmen, lawyers, architects, and government officials once stood barefoot on the plaza of La Florida
listening to reveille at dawn. One of those boys was Fernando,
who graduated from La Florida and went on to attend Yale
Medical School with the hope of becoming a physician. "I
would like to become a doctor, so I can give back some of what
I took away on the streets," he says humbly.

This extraordinary success has begun to transform the way a
lot of the people in Bogota view their gambinos. It has become
something of a badge of honor to have risen from the streets.
Two former presidents of Colombia now proudly admit they
were once gambinos.

Father Xavier is still listening to his children. Today, twenty-
five years after he first walked the streets with them, some

of today's children are saying they want to return to the countryside.

While thousands of children have found jobs in the city, Bogota, like any Third World city suffers from high unemployment. Many of the graduates of La Florida see their future not in the city, but on the land.

The result of hearing this message is the largest and most innovative effort in the world to counteract the mistakes of history that drew peasant farmers out of the mountains and into the city in the first place. Father Xavier has acquired from the Colombian government 250,000 acres of land in Tapparo, an uninhabited region of Colombia along the Orinoco River. There in the Amazon Basin, he is returning hundreds of children to their agrarian roots. With a grant from an American foundation, they built an agricultural school and set up advanced training programs to teach them how to live off of the land. The river is filled with fish that provide plenty of protein. Using satellite photography they have identified the most fertile soil and American universities have helped select which crops can sustain the pioneers and also be sold on the world market to generate cash.

There are already hundreds of young men and growing families living in Tapparo, and over the next few years, there are plans to build one thousand homes. It is all happening through a meeting of the minds.

Chapter Eight

No Narrators,
No Correspondents,
No Ambulances

You can't not let me give
when I know this show
is the reason I'm here.

AWARENESS OF THE INTERPLAY between the twin hemispheres of human thought became an important element in the production of the television series. Television is a medium dominated by people with advanced technological skills. If you sit around the lunch table in any production house in America, you're likely to hear a lot more conversation about gismos and gadgets than imagination and creativity. Moreover, the people who own the tools necessary to produce a television program are, more often than not, number crunchers whose livelihoods depend on their ability to sell their technology for a specific amount of money per hour. If you tried to think up an activity that required the most left-brained skills, you couldn't come up with a better example than someone who trades money (value reduced to a number) for technology (the concrete product of logic) for a specific amount of time (the ultimate objective lineal concept).

Since it was apparent from the very beginning that the programs would have to be put together with about 20 percent of the amount ordinarily spent on such projects, other resources besides cash would have to be used. This meant that if *Visionaries* was to become anything more than an idea, the first step would be to find someone to donate the technology.

The seminarians' band *Horizonte de Nueva Vida* joins the Visionaries crew (clockwise from top) Elizabeth Boland, Bruce Lundeen, John Capellupo and Bill Mosher.

Visionaries cameraman Bruce Lundeen in Cité Soleil, Haiti.

Outside of Boston, in Quincy, Massachusetts, the hometown of two presidents of the United States, John Adams and his son, John Quincy Adams, there are two large identical office buildings that straddle the border between Quincy and the town of Braintree. Most of the people who work inside the twin six-story structures of polished stone and glass are employed by a huge financial management company that invests other people's money for a fee. The women all wear smart dresses and the men suits and ties so that they look professional when they talk to clients on the phone or when they are sitting in front of a computer screen.

In 1993, a corner of one of the buildings was being leased to a small production company called Horizon Media. It was strictly a business relationship: Horizon needed a home with a corporate address since their clientele was mostly large companies. Nonetheless the normal attire at Horizon was dungarees and T-shirts. The company was owned by a partnership between two men. John Capellupo, the stout, good-hearted only son of Italian immigrants, ran the business end of the operation. Peter Huston, a tall, transplanted Ohioan with a salt-and-pepper beard, handled the production end of the company.

As is the case of any small company, however, the lines of responsibilities overlap and intersect more often than they follow neat flow charts or clear job descriptions. Although Peter was a producer, he was also the closest thing the company had to an account executive who serviced existing clients and went out and found new work. He could also shoot a camera, edit tape, and light a set. John, besides doubling as business manager and production coordinator, was also the in-house audio expert. Before forming the company, one of his previous incarnations was setting up sound systems for rock concerts in big sites like Foxboro Stadium. In a pinch, he could also shoot a camera and play the saxophone.

Rounding out the company was Jeff Rhind, one of the best technical video editors on the East coast. They call him Jeffrey Scissorhands, because when you order up a complicated edit, all you see is Jeff from behind, surrounded by his curving console of monitors and scopes; he nods, pauses for a second to think, then in a sudden burst of flailing hands and pounding keys, a foot or two of videotape is figuratively sliced to shreds. He reclines in his high-back swivel chair as the decks recoil at the barrage of commands; then after a moment they catch up and Jeff says over his shoulder, "Is that what you had in mind?" as the monitors reveal a work of art within the sixty frames that make up two seconds of video tape.

These are the people who made *Visionaries* work. By donating their equipment, their time, and their rare combination of skills, it suddenly seemed possible to produce a thirty-minute program on a budget with only a fifth of the money usually needed. If you ask them today why they did it, the answer might surprise you. They'll say they had a "feeling" it might work.

In 1993, Horizon Media, like every small production company in New England, was struggling. The large corporations for whom they produced training films and presentation videos were cutting back. Many, if not most, of Horizon's competitors had already gone out of business or were in some form of insolvency. Horizon survived because they tended to make instinctive decisions based on their "feel" for a project. They never did market analysis, wrote business plans for prospective projects, or conducted customer surveys in order to put together a strategic plan.

Even though they had two spare rooms, John and Peter shared a small office in the back of the suite. There they made decisions and planned their work with phones cradled on their shoulders and a stack of unpaid bills covering their desk tops.

When the idea for *Visionaries* came through the door one day, neither man even had a passport, never mind any experience shooting a program set primarily in foreign locales. John Capellupo, however, never hesitated a minute. He embraced the idea instantly and became the primary force behind putting together the resources needed to do the show. He donated one of the spare offices so *Visionaries* could have a home, and he installed a separate phone line and paid the bill. He picked up the cost of secretarial support, shipping dozens of promotional packets, and he provided free production services during the early days when there was no money at all.

When the funding was secured to shoot the first program on the American Liver Foundation, John, Peter, and Jeff carried beepers twenty-four hours a day and kept a camera kit on standby waiting for the call from the Grasso family. When the time came, it was John and Peter who left their families on a Sunday night and drove to a nearby airport with the equipment. En route, Peter and John flipped a coin to see who would do the shoot. It's a matter of opinion who won, but Peter squeezed his 6'3" frame into the four-seater to embark on the shoot that would require him to stand in an operating room for ten and a half hours. He was never paid for his camera work.

John Capellupo, who once played saxophone in his high school marching band, never planned a career in international television production. His first job was teaching computer science in his hometown, where he later opened a video store, met and married a local girl, and settled down to raise a family. Later, Peter Huston, who was working in the town's community cable station, stopped into the video store. Soon, they were building a production studio in the back room of the store. Before long, they sold off the movie rental business and headed into television production full time.

They never had a real plan; they just had a "feeling" it would all work out. A few years later, they found themselves standing in a trash-strewn dark alley in Colombia that reeked of urine and rotting garbage. They spent a week surrounded by a horde of Colombian street children, most of whom were armed with knives. One of their guides, a former street kid, casually admitted to having killed thirteen people. It was a long way from the small town on the South Shore of Massachusetts, but they took it all in stride.

John, who became *Visionaries'* biggest supporter, also traveled to Kenya, Mozambique, Haiti, and El Salvador. Peter worked to keep Horizon going while John dedicated more and more time to *Visionaries,* but he did manage to squeeze in trips to the Philippines, Appalachia, and the Pine Ridge Indian Reservation in South Dakota.

With the completion of each program, more and more people began to get the "feeling" that *Visionaries* just might work even though the Discovery Channel, Lifetime, A & E, TNT, and virtually every agent, syndicator, and media consultant in the country rejected *Visionaries*.

A clear delineation appeared between those who rallied to *Visionaries*' support and those who backed away. Those who wanted no part of the project usually never actually watched an episode and rejected the concept because it did not fit neatly into any existing category of programing. It didn't have a narrator, so it couldn't be a documentary. There was no correspondent, so it wasn't news. The shows didn't have any cops or ambulances, so it couldn't be reality programing. Besides, good news didn't sell.

The supporters were people like Elizabeth Boland. She was a CPA and the former comptroller of one of the largest home health care companies in America. When her company was bought out, she accepted a severance package that allowed her to take some time off and reflect on what she really wanted to do with her life. She was only thirty-five but had already experienced what it was like at the top of the corporate ladder and wasn't impressed or fulfilled by either the money or the so-called prestige.

Born in Colorado to parents who were both CPAs, she naturally gravitated to the structure and security some people find in large companies. After graduating from Notre Dame, she worked for companies like Price Waterhouse, but all the while there was a part of her that longed for creative fulfillment. She explored this part of her personality by singing in a jazz band and studying art.

It was her interest in the history of art that put her on a British Airways flight bound for Rome in May of 1994. On the first leg of the trip from Boston to London, she was in an aisle seat in the last row in the center section. Sitting in the other three seats were three men bound for Africa. The one sitting beside her was trying to make the best of yet another airline nightmare. Because the seats were against the rear wall, they did not recline, making it difficult to sleep on the overnight flight. The video machine was broken so movies were not an option, and the electrical system had short circuited, making it impossible to read without the cabin lights. He said to himself, "There has to be a reason for this," and turned to the woman beside him and mumbled a question about her destination. She explained that she was going to tour the museums in Rome.

They talked for a little over an hour as the man told her that he was part of a television crew that was going to Africa to shoot a documentary for a new series called *Visionaries*. There was something about the story the man told that fascinated her. In a way, it seemed like the dream job, traveling around the world, living and working with people who didn't care about money, but who found the kind of personal fulfillment that had always seemed to elude her. They exchanged phone numbers. Today, Elizabeth Boland is a *Visionaries* associate producer. When she came back from Rome, she came on board as a volunteer. Elizabeth now handles all the organization's administrative responsibilities when she is not on the road as a member of the shooting team.

There were scores of other people who heard about what *Visionaries* was doing and stepped forward to help out. Most of them were moved to action after seeing one of the episodes. Since one of the goals of the *Visionaries* project was to leave each organization with a tool it could use to fulfill its mission, long before broadcast became a reality, the programs were being shown in private venues all over the world. Joe Kilpatrick, assistant director to the Z. Smith Reynolds Foundation, was sitting in the audience for a showing of the Human Service Alliance program and was stunned by what he saw. In all his years working in the non-profit world, he had never seen a presentation that captured the very essence of volunteer work in such a powerful and emotion-evoking manner. He took it upon himself to let the higher echelons of the non-profit world know about *Visionaries* and to challenge them to step forward and help the project. He arranged a series of meetings in Washington with groups like the Council on Foundations, the Independent Sector, and the Benton Foundation, all major players in the philanthropic community. From the time he saw his first *Visionaries* episode, Joe Kilpatrick would go anywhere, call anyone, and do anything he could to help bring *Visionaries* to the air.

Over time, things began to come together in a way no one could ever have planned. What might have appeared to be a series of unrelated events coincided to create the elements necessary to convince the skeptical world of television that there might be something to this *Visionaries* program.

When the completed program featuring Judy Mayotte was presented to the board of directors of Refugees International at a country lodge in suburban Virginia, something strange happened. The audience of thirty people sat in stunned silence for a full five minutes after the large-screen television went black. Their eyes were filled with tears and they seemed unable to speak as a wave of emotion washed over them. Finally, Bill Clark, the chairman of the board, broke the silence. For the next two hours, the group reflected on how much Judy had sacrificed for their common cause, and for a while, at least, they looked at their work in a new light.

Not long after the meeting, Bill Clark called the actor Sam Waterston to tell him about *Visionaries*. Throughout his entire career, Sam had built a reputation as an actor committed to quality programing. He had become involved with Refugees International when he was making the movie *The Killing Fields*. Bill Clark sent him a copy of the program. After one look, he volunteered to help *Visionaries* in any way he could. He flew to Boston at his own expense and donated his time to shoot the opening of four programs that would be presented to a PBS distributor for consideration. The same distributor had all but rejected the program because it was too emotional and it lacked the traditional narration. Sam Waterston changed everyone's mind.

At about the same time, a woman by the name of Kate Billings was going through the kind of ambivalence about her career that Elizabeth Boland had experienced. She had worked in the public broadcasting community for over nineteen years and finally quit her senior producer's job at WETA in Washington after feeling unfulfilled. As part of her quest for a job that had meaning, she attended a weekend retreat in the Boston area called Life/Work Direction. After the session had ended, she was sitting in the living room with the couple who operated the retreat. Kate Billings's hosts told her a story about a successful graphic artist who had worked in the Boston area and who had given up all of her clients and moved to North Carolina to live and work in a facility that cared for the terminally ill. They pulled out a video cassette and told her about this extraordinary program that captured the essence of volunteerism. Later, Kate watched the rough-cut version of the *Visionaries* episode profiling the Human Service Alliance. Although she had worked most of her adult life in the television industry and thought she had seen everything that the medium had to offer, she was deeply moved by what she saw. The episode seemed to embody all of the things she thought television should be about. The next day, she sat down and prepared a long, handwritten letter to the producers of the program offering to help in any way she could.

In a telephone conversation the next week, Kate Billings was told that *Visionaries*, after a year of work, still had not found a broadcast or cable outlet. That same day, she began calling everybody she could think of who could help. Within a month, she had introduced the program to WGBH in Boston. The flagship station of the 350-member public broadcasting network quickly decided to lend their support by attaching their name to the project and presenting it to the rest of the network in a national satellite feed. It was the first time in years that the most prestigious PBS station in the country had supported an independent production in this manner.

A few months later, Kate Billings packed her bags and moved to Boston to volunteer full-time on the staff of *Visionaries*. She had been living off her savings since leaving WETA the previous year. In the beginning, *Visionaries* had no money to pay her and she couldn't afford to take an apartment, so she stayed with friends in the area so she could be a part of the project. When she arrived in Boston, she said, "Ever since I saw the first *Visionaries* episode, I knew in my heart this is where I was meant to be."

Jessica Locke, another volunteer who scored the music for the Human Service Alliance show, felt the same "sense of knowing" after watching a single episode of the series. *Visionaries* had no money to pay her either, particularly since the entire budget for that show was $10,000 provided by an anonymous donor. Despite extraordinary talent, Jessica's freelance music production business had suffered when the bottom fell out of the economy in Massachusetts. Ad agencies and production houses that once had the money to spend on original music now found it necessary to get by on canned music. Business was so bad that she finally had to close down her studio and move back to her father's farm in Ohio. When she arrived on the three-hundred-acre spread, there was a tremendous sense of sadness and an overwhelming feeling of disconnection from everything she thought was important in her life. Out of the darkest moment came a single thought. She picked up the phone and called *Visionaries*. She said there was only one thing she knew for sure in her life and that was that she was meant to do the music for *Visionaries*. The producer protested that they didn't have the money to pay her, and she of all people was not in a position to donate the enormous amount of time necessary to score the twelve remaining episodes. She put her foot down. "You can't not let me give when I know this show is the reason I'm here. I can just feel it."

CHAPTER NINE

Little Miracles

*As long as you put the needs
of the children first, everything
will work out in the end.*

J UST A FEW HUNDRED MILES northeast of Borneo, in the archipelago nation of the Philippines, is an island called Jolo. It is a tense, foreboding place where strangers stand out.

You're coming down the ramp of the Fokker sixty-seater, straining under the weight of the Sony Betacam video camera slung over your shoulder. The late morning sun pierces the thick humid air and cuts a path into your eyes. Before you are halfway across the soft crusty asphalt of the single runway, beads of sweat are running down your back and, no matter how hard you try, you can't seem to adjust your eyes to the intense light. Out of the wet blur, you see a figure approaching. He is backlit by the hot orange sun, but in his silhouette you make out the distinctive cut of a military-style uniform. There is a sidearm strapped to his waist and another weapon is held in both hands tightly against his chest.

"Who are you?" he demands in surprisingly good English. You begin to answer but he fires another question before the words can form. "What are you doing here?"

You stumble and he interrupts again, displaying his agitation and his surprise at the sight of a lone American invading his turf. You mumble something about shooting a documentary, and he stops you again in mid-sentence with another question that sounds more like a declaratory sentence.

"Are you crazy? Do you have any idea where you are? This is Jolo." Then he fires another question that you can answer. "Are you alone?"

137

"No," you respond, feeling a bit better that you are holding up your end of the conversation.

"Who are you with?" he asks, looking at the small group of passengers still deplaning, and then comments under his breath, "If they all look like you, you should all get back on the plane."

Finally, the people who have led you to this place step between you and the man with the gun. An argument ensues in which the police officer points out testily that the last strangers to visit the island two weeks earlier are still being held by terrorists.

Left unsaid is the story of the Catholic priest who was recently kidnapped from the altar while saying Mass in front of a church full of worshipers. It's a tale the government would like to forget since the Muslim rebels accomplished the audacious feat while the church was surrounded by government troops.

One of the men arguing on your behalf is Ed Lim, the director of a program for Muslim children orphaned by war. He is an important person in Jolo, and the officer gives in and allows the crew to pass through the chain link fence, under the condition that they report directly to the police station to arrange for protection.

Quickly, the crew is hustled into the back of an enclosed truck and driven away before too many people notice their arrival. The fewer people who know that a group of Americans is in town the better, at least that is what you were told in the security briefing held secretly in the back room of a hotel on the nearby island of Mindanao.

The truck races through the streets clogged with bicycles that have brightly painted sidecars welded to their frames. Through the small dirt-covered windows that afford the passengers their only view of the town, exotic images flicker past. Steaming kettles of hot food are offered out of roadside stands by veiled women. Men, wearing traditional Muslim headgear, rush about the marketplaces trading goods from push carts that are crowded down narrow alleys and clustered around the lime green mosque in the center of town.

On this island, which guards the confluence of the sister seas, the Sulu and the Celebes, two cultures merge. To the south is Indonesia, the largest Muslim nation on earth. To the north is the predominantly Catholic country of the Philippines, which lays claim to this forgotten place.

Here the north is represented by the government and spatterings of commercial enterprises stuffed inside the crude concrete buildings that fill the business district. The south, however, holds the heart and soul of the people, who share a feeling of being oppressed and dominated by a nationalistic power that takes their resources and returns little in the way of services.

The conflict reached a pinnacle of nightmarish violence in 1974 when President Ferdinand Marcos ordered gunboats to take up positions off the coast. The Moro National Liberation Front (MNLF) had been waging a long war against the government from their mountain stronghold located in the center of the island. Unable to ferret out the rebels, the government retaliated by unleashing a devastating barrage of cannon fire that leveled the town, destroying virtually every building and killing hundreds of people. When the troops landed, they took whomever they could find into custody. Some, like Ed Lim, were bound, blindfolded, and hustled off to a secret location where they were subjected to long, brutal interrogations that went on for days.

The truck swings out of the traffic and slides to a stop on a sandy embankment that descends toward a small inlet where crude boats made out of scrap lumber are tied to poles embedded in the muddy harbor floor. The strangers are hustled out of the truck and led along a walkway of wooden planks to the shore. The idea of reporting to the police station was never seriously contemplated. The pointed nose of a thirty-foot-long canoe-like craft, called a banca, is pulled up on shore and the group awkwardly makes their way on board, tiptoeing, with outstretched arms like tightrope walkers, toward the stern. An old gas-powered engine is coughing up puffs of blue smoke as it struggles not to stall. Along the shore, curious onlookers stare at the odd collection of foreigners. The boat is pushed away from land and makes a wide turn and heads out to sea.

Elizabeth Boland, the CPA who became involved with *Visionaries* after a chance meeting with the crew on a British Airways flight to Africa, is sitting in the middle of the boat with a blue scarf wrapped around her head in keeping with the Muslim tradition of the area. It is her first trip as a *Visionaries* volunteer. Sharing the wooden plank that serves as a seat is Bruce Lundeen, the man who has become *Visionaries'* primary cameraman, having cut his teeth shooting an episode in Haiti. He has the rare talent to be able to stand like a statue for twenty minutes and also be able to move fearlessly through dangerous terrain, walking backward with his only view of the world through his lens. One row up, sitting beside Peter Huston, who is handling audio on the trip, is the man who has led the crew on one of its most dangerous excursions. His name is Danny Urquico.

Danny's round face is warm and open and his sleepy eyes and sad jowls accentuate his calm demeanor. He was born in Baguio, five and a half hours north of Manila. His mother was a member of a minority tribe from outside the city. His father was an American serviceman of Italian descent who deserted him, his mother, and his sister when his tour of duty was up. Not long afterward, Danny's mother died of a heart attack, and he became an orphan at the age of two. He was one of the lucky ones, however. A wealthy family took him under their wing and eventually adopted him, raising him in an atmosphere of love and affection. Still, however, there lingered a gnawing sense that he did not belong. He was ostracized in school because of his ethnic heritage, which only increased the sense of abandonment that ate away at his self-esteem. Despite the unswerving support given to him by his adoptive parents, he drifted into drugs and eventually became one of the biggest drug dealers in the Philippines. He spent his share of nights in jail before finding the road out. He met the woman who became his wife and found the kind of emotional fulfillment that had eluded him for so long. Once he got clear of the drug subculture, he began to see how truly lucky he had been.

With this came the realization that there were thousands of
kids on the street who were struggling to survive without the
kind of support from which he had benefited. He committed
himself to helping those kids. In the beginning, he tried to fill
the role played by other men in his life who had come along
at critical times to fill the gap left by his biological father, men
like his tae kwon do coach.

He started recreation and sports programs for street kids
and got involved in counseling. Once he made the commitment to be part of the solution, a series of events occurred that
he would later call the little miracles that changed his life.

Twenty minutes out to sea, a ragged line of strange structures
appear on the horizon not far off the shore of a small island.
As the boat plugs along, the water turns azure blue while the
sandy bottom comes into view. Slowly, you begin to make out
the outline of a community of stilt houses that look like a flock
of weary four-legged creatures wading out to sea.

The engine putters to a crawl and the long boat turns in
an arc, entering a small enclosure surrounded by the nipa-
thatched huts built out of strips of bamboo and side-walled
with matted coconut leaves. These are the homes of the Badjaos, a simple, gentle people who have lived for centuries on
the ocean. They are called the sea gypsies and are among the
most marginalized and least understood people on earth.

Colonies of Badjaos can be found throughout the Philippines, but no matter where they go, they are greeted with
disdain and often outright hostility. Even here, one of the
southernmost outposts, they are victimized. Roving bands of
pirates attack the men when they leave the safety of the
colony to fish. When the children tried to attend a school located on a nearby island, they were taunted by the classmates
and physically assaulted by the teachers. On the rare occasions
when they must go to Jolo, for supplies or to seek medical help
for their children, they are exploited and often robbed of what
few possessions they own.

Over the centuries, the children who live on the land have been told that if they did not behave, the Badjaos would come in the middle of the night and steal them. In the Philippines, you grow into adulthood believing that the Badjaos are dirty, uncivilized transients who steal what they can and move on before they can be caught. The demonization of the Badjaos is so universally accepted that it is thought that the word "boogieman" finds its origins as a derivative of the word "Badjao."

At the sound of the approaching engine, thin, pretty women carrying infants step out onto the bamboo decks to greet the visitors with shy smiles. Children take to the water, paddling in tubs and wash basins toward the canoe, giggling with excitement. In the shallow water, fingerlings dart over the sandbar that is covered with a thick layer of fish bones, collected over the years after being tossed out of the huts.

Every window, doorway, and deck is now filled with people who have come out of their homes to witness the arrival of the visitors from some far-off land. You look up from the canoe and scan the smiling faces, and when you make eye contact, each person blushes and then raises a hand to wave sheepishly.

At the head of the tiny harbor is the largest structure in the barrio of over 150 houses that teeter precariously above the sandbar in an irregular trail over a quarter-mile long. This building is a two-room school house that has changed the lives of the three hundred families who live in this passage between two seas.

Over the centuries, the Badjaos have wandered the oceans practicing animism while maintaining a nominal adherence to the Muslim religion that dominates the area. The fundamental tenet of their way of life is a deep commitment to peace. When conflict arises, their nature is to simply go away. Their lives are symbolized by the single possession that is common to every Badjao home: a battered suitcase that holds all of the family's possessions. They are a quiet, shy people who have lived on boats for hundreds of years so they could sail away from conflict at a moment's notice. It is only recently that they have begun planting sticks in the ocean floor and building boathouses in one place. Even this is a tenuous commitment that varies from one band of Badjao to another. Some in this community that goes by the name of Suba Suba, which means sea passage, have been in the area for barely a generation.

Living twenty minutes off the coast of Jolo has not changed their ways. They still refuse to put up walls inside their houses, which are shared by two or three families, because they believe that the partitions will offend the spirits of their dead ancestors. And young children are still taught to deal with anger and frustration in a way that is uniquely Badjaoan. They break into spontaneous song.

After you climb out of the banca and scale the ladder that leads up into the school house, the sound of children chanting rhythmically fills the air. You follow the mystical sound that is coming from the classroom in the back of the building. There, in front of the blackboard, a little girl dressed in a polka-dot skirt is gently stomping her feet to the beat of the music as her arms curl away from her body in a slow, trance-like gesture. Beams of sunlight reflect up through the slatted floor, illuminating the child in thin stripes of light as she turns in a circle in front of the classroom filled with singing children. She stares straight ahead with a serenely confident look on her face that seems to express an inner calm.

The Badjao children could not get through their school day without their songs. The reason is that these are no ordinary students. They are the first Badjaos in the entire community of fifteen hundred to learn to read and write.

How that came to happen and how a former drug dealer from Baguio became involved with the project is a remarkable story of what can happen when you involve yourselves in the details of helping other people and allowing the magic to happen.

The story begins in Hawaii in 1967. At the time, very few people in the social service community were talking about the issue of abused children, except for a lone social worker by the name of Patti Lyons. She was working for the Child and Family Service Organization and was assigned to an area of Honolulu with the lowest income and the highest crime rate in the state. It seemed like every day she would come in contact with another case of physical and sexual abuse. The images of children bruised and beaten that were preserved in snapshots taken as evidence began to haunt her. Finally, she came to the conclusion that the only solution to the problem was to speak out publicly and address what she perceived to be a growing crisis. The public responded with outrage. Some rallied to the cause and joined her crusade to build a shelter for abused children. Others, however, felt that the issue was being sensationalized and exaggerated. They called for Patti Lyons to be removed as a social worker.

It was a long and difficult fight that required the public to look at a side of humanity that turned their view of their own lives upside down and threatened to tear apart the image they had about their culture. Finally, the state of Hawaii opened the first Child Protective Service Center for abused children in its history and one of the first of its kind in the nation. Patti Lyons was invited to speak at the ribbon-cutting ceremony. Five years later, the national organization that was petitioned by opponents to remove her license to practice social work named her the first Hawaiian National Social Worker of the Year.

Patti Lyons learned an important lesson in the turmoil created by her campaign on the behalf of children victimized by sexual and physical abuse: that as long as you put the needs of the children first, everything will work out in the end.

It was that philosophy that got her through the next great challenge in her life. In her job with Child and Family Service, one program she administered was processing adoptions of children from the Philippines by Hawaiian families. Although the rewards of the work were enormous, she was confronted by the fact that millions of children in the Philippines desperately

Patti Lyons "hears children cry" and has dedicated her life to help them in the Philippines and Hawaii.

Badjao village children dance at their new school above the water in Jolo, Sulu, the Philippines.

needed services. The act of plucking a few lucky children out of poverty seemed to bring into focus their level of need. Then one day she was challenged by Corazon de Leon — currently a secretary and cabinet member of President Ramos — who asked her why she continued to take away the country's greatest asset, its children, and didn't do anything to help those left behind. She decided to answer the question by making a commitment to find a way to help the children of the Philippines. Once the commitment was made, a series of events occurred that would result in the development of one of the most remarkable programs ever created for the children of both the Philippines and Hawaii.

Patti received a telephone call from a Filipino woman living in Hawaii who was inquiring about adoptions. The call should have gone to the adoption unit but was somehow misdirected to her desk. The woman told her a story about a man who lived in Baguio who was working with street children. A short time later a letter arrived on Patti's desk. It was from Danny Urquico, the same man described by the woman inquiring about adoptions. It was another one of those strange coincidences that Patti had come to see as miracles guiding her way.

In the letter Danny explained that he had started sports and recreation programs that provided homeless kids with a place to go during the day. Now he was trying to find help in setting up a shelter that would get them off the street permanently. The next time Patti was in the Philippines, she arranged to meet Danny Urquico.

When Patti arrived in Baguio, Danny waited until midnight to take her out into the streets to meet the children that came to his programs during the day. They went to a site near the marketplace where the children lived in holes burrowed in the side of a mountain. Rats scurried about, competing with the children for the scraps of garbage tossed out by the fruit and vegetable vendors. One four-year-old boy was pulled out of a garbage can where he had been sleeping. His body was covered with sores that had become infected by the thick grime that covered his little body. Patti focused on that one child for a moment and looked into his big round eyes and saw the simplicity of what needed to be done. This boy, and all the children like him, needed a place to live. She did not know how it would happen, but she knew she was going to take the first step into the unknown and go wherever the road took her. That first step was to challenge the children to become a part of the solution. She and Danny told them that if they really wanted help, they should meet them back at the marketplace the following day. Thirty kids showed up. Patti asked them what was the single thing they most wanted in life. There was no debate. The children said they wanted to go to school. They wanted a chance at a better life.

Patti returned to her job thousands of miles away in Hawaii, but her mind was on the Philippines. At the same time, unbeknown to either Patti Lyons or Danny Urquico, there was a third person who also had spent a lot of time thinking about the needs of children on the two tiny specks of real estate thousands of miles apart. Her name was Doña Consuelo Alger.

Mrs. Alger's family, the Zobel de Ayalas, had been among the aristocracy in the Philippines for over four hundred years. When she was young, she fell in love with a young American army officer, James Dyce Alger. After they married, she traveled with him as he climbed the military ladder to become a general. Finally, they settled in Hawaii on the island where Patti worked. As the years went by, Consuelo longed for her homeland and developed a deep yearning to fill the void left in her own life by the fact that she and her husband never had any children of their own.

She heard about the work that Patti Lyons was doing and sent her a note requesting a meeting. Patti told Consuelo about what she had seen on the streets of Consuelo's country and about Danny Urquico, the child of an American army officer and Filipino woman who himself ended up an orphan.

Consuelo offered to help. She provided the money to buy a building in Baguio to serve as a shelter for street children and pledged her long-term financial support for the program.

The little four-year-old boy whom Danny and Patti had

found living in a trash can was one of the first to move into the new home, nestled in a cool grove of trees on a hill above the city. As the program took shape, two of the children traveled to Hawaii and were able to spend some time with Consuelo.

One day Consuelo called Patti to another meeting. The proud, regal lady had developed bladder cancer that later spread to the brain. She told Patti that she had only one wish. She "wanted to spend her heaven doing good on earth." Therefore, she had decided to create a foundation to guarantee the continued support of the work they had begun together. She wanted to leave something eternal.

When she died on November 29, 1990, the eternal gift she left behind for the children of the Philippines and Hawaii was a foundation bearing her name. Virtually all of her wealth, most of which was in the form of stock in the family-owned Ayala Corporation, was left to the foundation. The total value of her gift is estimated to be more than $100 million.

The concept of finding a measure of immortality by endowing a foundation is not a new idea. Many of the major industrialists of the twentieth century placed huge fortunes in trusts for specific philanthropic purposes. Thousands of charitable programs are funded every year by using only the interest on part of the enormous wealth accumulated during the lifetimes of people like Henry Ford, J. Paul Getty, and Robert Wood Johnson, the founder of Johnson & Johnson.

Doña Consuelo's decision to "spend her heaven doing good on earth" does, however, reveal a new phenomenon within the world of giving that has gone virtually unnoticed. We think of foundations as being stuffy institutions that dole out grants from wood-paneled boardrooms occupied by cigar-smoking bankers. Something much more dynamic is going on in America. In the decade after 1980, a full third of the country's thirty-two thousand foundations came into existence. These ten thousand new organizations stimulated a 93 percent increase in the amount of assets held by foundations to bring the total to nearly $140 billion. What this means is that a thousand new foundations are forming every year, building an ever-increasing nest egg that is being held in trust for the sole purpose of helping people. These new foundations and the amount of money they are putting in the bank for non-profit purposes is stimulating a growth in the foundation world that is more than twice the rate of inflation. Today, if you were to divide the money up evenly among the more than a million non-profit organizations in the country, every one of them would get over $100,000. Add to this the untold billions of dollars that are left to non-profit organizations in individual bequests, trusts, and wills and you discover that a silent trend is emerging.

In a recent study, people in their nineties were asked what would they do differently if they had an opportunity to live their lives over again. They listed three changes they would make. First, they would spend more time with their families. Second, they would take more risks in their lives. The third thing they would have done differently was to live their lives so that they could leave something behind . . . something eternal.

What Consuelo Alger left behind is helping to support the first school house built among the Badjaos. So far, over two hundred children have already learned to read and write. Now their parents are coming to the bamboo boathouse to attend class so they can keep up with their children. What this means in practical terms is that the world outside of their barrio no longer appears to be a place of open hostility. They now have bank books with their own names on them. When they go into town they can read the street signs, enter into business contracts, borrow money to purchase fishing equipment, and arrange for medical care for their children. This interaction with the outside world is beginning to change the perception people have of the Badjaos as they develop relationships with more and more people who live in the strange houses in the ocean. A tiny, almost imperceptible portion of Consuelo Alger's eternal gift has changed their lives forever.

The same kind of magic is occurring in the center of Jolo in the program created by Ed Lim and supported by the Alger Foundation.

It's after midnight. You're curled up on a thin mat in a dark corner of a classroom on the fourth floor of the facility that Ed Lim operates in the heart of Jolo. You can't sleep. Strange noises echo up from the street and climb through the open window over your head and then bounce about in the empty room. There is the sound of a chinging bell, like the one a child might have on a bicycle. It seems to be coming from across the street in the deserted courtyard around the mosque. There is a man out there hawking his wares to a sleeping city. Or is that just a cover — an excuse to be across the street from the building that houses the foolish Americans stupid enough to spend the night in Jolo?

Every once in a while you pick up the sound of a lone car winding its way through the city streets. You follow the noise intently, trying to judge whether it is coming in your direction. The closer it gets, the more you realize how easy it would be for a small band of terrorists with automatic weapons to kick in the front door and storm up the stairs — certainly a lot easier than snatching a priest off of the altar in a church surrounded by armed guards.

That, after all, was the point the chief of police was trying to make when he showed up with six rifle-toting guards in tow after your return from the Badjaos. After intercepting you on the stairs, the soldiers escorted you into the dining room where the plainclothes chief stood with his hands clasped behind his back, staring out the window to the street below. He began to speak without turning around, demanding to know where you had been all day. Then, like a cannon atop a turret, he swung around slowly. He looked like something out of a Rambo movie: cold, steely black eyes, a little mouth, and strong chiseled jaw that made his small, muscular frame seem more formidable.

Even when you extended your hand, his sunken, pock-marked cheeks didn't give a hint of cordiality. The only time he seemed at all amused was when he caught you staring at the huge handgun stuck inside a brown leather shoulder holster. He wore it on the outside of his street clothes like a badge of honor, seemingly oblivious to the idea that shoulder holsters were designed to conceal weapons.

"You must leave Jolo immediately," he demanded. "This place is not safe for strangers."

For a moment, you entertained the idea of telling him about the secret meeting that reportedly occurred earlier in the week between your hosts and a representative of the rebel faction, but then you weren't sure how true the story was in the first place. After all, if the rebels had agreed to guarantee your safety, as was suggested, why were there always two men with forty-five caliber handguns watching over you like mother hens?

After a round of tea and a placating promise to leave the island first thing in the morning, the chief went away. A simple call to the airport would have revealed that the crew was scheduled to leave on the first flight in the morning anyway.

Now a loud metallic voice bellows out a melodic prayer from the loudspeakers set in the tower of the mosque. You contemplate putting in the ear plugs you carry with you for just such situations, but then you wonder what would be worse, losing a few hours sleep or not hearing the sound of men storming through the building in search of fresh hostages. You lie awake listening to the prayer and wondering what it must be like for Ed Lim and the people who work with him. Earlier in the night, he had sat with you on the roof of the building and, looking out over the city, talked about his dream of ending the cycle of violence that was devouring his people.

"The people in this world who use the Koran to justify their violence do not know the Koran. Violence is un-Islamic. Islam is about peace — peace with yourself, peace with your neighbor, and peace with God. This is what we are teaching the victims of war. Then maybe we can break the cycle of violence."

Ed Lim is an intense man in a compact body who looks at you through thin, wire-rimmed glasses with soft, insightful eyes. There are six hundred young children who come to his program every day. The girls wear bluish-green veils and the boys balance traditional white turbans on their heads as they file happily into the classroom that now doubles as your bedroom. All of the children have lost at least one parent in the war. This is not an orphanage, however; it is an outreach program that provides families that have been victimized by war with the support to stay together. Even if children have lost both parents, they live with aunts and uncles or even older siblings. This is the way of Islam.

In partnership with the Alger Foundation, Ed Lim and his staff of volunteers provide the children with an education that teaches seven subjects, including English. They provide support for the widows at home and help older children learn the skills necessary to find employment. All the while, everything they do is in accordance with the Islamic tradition.

The great danger that is presented by so many children orphaned by war is that their loss will be turned into rage, creating yet another generation of victims. The Koran says that if you kill someone, you are killing your brother and sister. Ed Lim wants that cycle to end in Jolo by teaching the children most affected by the war that peace can come only through forgiveness.

All over the Philippines, the gift left by Consuelo is having a profound impact on people of dramatically different backgrounds.

There is a place on the outskirts of Manila called Smoky Mountain. It is not really a mountain. It is a giant pile of trash that covers over one hundred acres of land along a putrid river that flows like an open sewer toward the ocean. This smoldering landfill is also the home of thirty-five hundred families who live in the trash, in homes built out of trash, who often earn their living by picking through the trash.

To reach Smoky Mountain you must travel down a long dusty road that is clogged by a seemingly endless row of trash trucks overflowing with the discards from the eight million people who live and work in Manila. The ocean is on the left, somewhere behind a half-mile-long, thirty-foot-high wall of garbage. If you poke your head out the window of your car, you can look up and see people crawling across the plateau of rotting refuse that is steaming in the hot sun. They're methodically picking through the garbage looking for anything that can be salvaged — pieces of metal, scraps of plastic, a morsel of food here, and a table scrap there.

On the right side of the road, shacks are built precariously, one atop the other, climbing up the mountain slope. Some have roofs of corrugated tin; most are topped with overlapping layers of anything flat. Near the end of the road there is an opening between the shanty homes, and an alleyway snakes up a hill. Danny climbs out of his jeep. At his side is a Catholic priest who has lived in the trash with these people for fifteen years. His name is Father Ben, and he is a scholar educated in Rome who decided his place was among the poor. Like Father Xavier in Colombia, he is a member of the Salesian order, whose specialty is providing educational and vocational services to the poorest of the poor.

Danny and Father Ben are heading for the church he has built among the poor. He has created a program that has taken one thousand kids from Smoky Mountain and taught them to be mechanics, computer technicians, and office workers. Father Ben and other members of the Salesian order working in the Philippines have formed a partnership with the Alger Foundation to expand services to try to reach out to the more than fifty thousand children living on the streets.

As they walk down the alley that weaves deeper and deeper into this hidden community, an odd change in perspective occurs. Viewing the place from a passing car creates an almost overwhelming sense of despair, if not horror, at what these people have been forced to endure. But here on the ground, walking shoulder to shoulder with the people, the impression is amazingly different. Every window and doorway seems to be filled with smiling faces. Children run up and tag along, giggling at the sight of the video camera. As you linger, young mothers holding children smile and welcome you into the cardboard boxes and refrigerator crates they call home. You peek inside and see spotlessly clean little rooms with plastic bucket stools, car seat couches, and tables made out of discarded wire spools.

"When people from the outside come here they are surprised to see the harmony and sense of community that exists on Smoky Mountain. The crime rate is very low here. Everyone looks out for everyone else," Father Ben says.

Once you look beyond the trash, a different picture does emerge. You begin to notice that everyone seems to be washing something. Clean clothes hang from lines strung between the huts, and teenagers are in the street, made of packed trash, sweeping it clean.

Danny pauses for a moment and takes a long tug on one of the cigarettes he wishes he didn't smoke. "You look around a place like this and you can begin to understand what our work is about. Consuelo's vision was about hope and dignity. She wanted to bring those two things to the poorest of the poor. Look into the faces of these people. They are living under the worst conditions imaginable but they are happy, loving people. Why? Because they have hope. Father Ben has brought them that feeling that life can get better. Our role at Alger is to form partnerships with people like this and give them the resources they need to succeed."

Seven thousand miles away on the island of Honolulu, people in dramatically different circumstances are witnessing the incredible power the vision of a single person can have on the lives of others.

The spirit of Consuelo and the practical idealism of Patti Lyons are having an impact all over Hawaii in programs like the foundation's Healthy and Ready to Learn Program.

In a recent survey of children in the geographic area around this program, it was discovered that a full third were not "ready to learn." What this meant is that they lacked basic conceptual skills like the ability to recognize colors and numbers. Others had poor attention spans and seemed stunted in their ability to grasp some simple ideas necessary for learning. It was determined that many of these problems were the result of problems in the home during early childhood. Due in large part to the existence of stress in the households, children were not able to receive the kind of care and attention needed to stimulate growth. Some were isolated from playmates and didn't develop social skills; others did not have access to books and toys that would help in early development. Some parents were living in such intense and abusive situations that they simply could not parent adequately.

Everyone seemed to agree that the key was early intervention. The Hawaii Family Stress Center had already instituted a statewide screening program called "Healthy Start." Every new parent was asked to fill out a questionnaire designed to help identify those who might be "environmentally at risk." Problems like crowded housing, acute poverty, drug and alcohol addiction, and a score of other stressful situations that could interfere with effective parenting were looked for closely. Once a family that might need help was identified, they were then referred to Alger's Healthy and Ready to Learn Program.

Here, in the brightly lit building with colorful walls, young families are offered an array of services that support them through the early years of development. There is free medical care, parenting classes, play groups, and trained social workers to work with each family individually. In this environment, young parents with similar problems bond together, and begin to understand that they are not alone. This interaction between young mothers stimulates a sense of shared experience, and together, they benefit from specific elements of the program as well as from the sense of being part of something larger.

Not far away, another program, whose entire budget is derived from Consuelo's gift, is establishing a whole new generation of hope.

The average cost of a single family home on this island is $315,000. Many of the families who have lived here since before the beginning of recorded history are forced to make a choice between moving to the mainland or living in poverty. It is not just a question of never being able to own a home. The shortage of housing has caused rents to soar as high as a $1,000 or more for a two bedroom apartment. Since many of the young families earn only $20,000 a year, having their own place to live is often out of the question. The result is that they are forced to live with relatives in intensely overcrowded units built on marginal land. The anger, frustration, and resentment that come from being forced further and further down the economic ladder have had a profound impact on the island's once peaceful culture. Drugs, violent crime, child abuse, and alcoholism are now as common here as in the big cities on the mainland.

During the few short years that Patti Lyons and Consuelo Alger worked together, Consuelo shared with Patti her dreams for the future, knowing they could come true only after she was gone. These concepts and ideas were broad impressions of how life ought to be for the children and families of the world. The beauty of their relationship was that Patti, after more than thirty years' experience in the social service system, knew how to take those abstract concepts and create programs that would make the dreams come true.

Consuelo saw the very fabric of Hawaiian culture threatened by a disintegration of the family unit and dreamed of a place where children and families could live in secure, tight-knit communities, free of drugs and violence. In her mind's eye, she pictured children laughing and playing in a neighborhood where everyone knew and cared about each other. She envisioned that some day they would then give back to their community what had been given to them.

Patti took that pretty picture, and along with her longtime friend and colleague, Caroline Oda, she began to build a program that would make it come true. An essential component of this planning process was incorporating the lessons that Patti and Caroline had learned from working on the front lines of the Child and Family Service sector for so many years.

They understood, for example, that many social service programs failed when the recipients of the service were not vested in the process. They sought, therefore, to build a program that would forge an equal relationship between the foundation and the families who desperately needed a place to live.

The Alger Foundation purchased a parcel of unused farm land in 1992 to help fulfill a dream that Patti and Consuelo shared before her death. The acreage was subdivided, and the necessary roads and utilities were built by the foundation. The next step was to find a small number of families that wanted to invest their time and energy in building a community. Five hundred such families applied to be included in the program. Out of this initial group, one hundred families participated in counseling sessions conducted by the foundation to help them prepare family budgets and submit applications to local banks for mortgages of $50,000. That amount represented the actual cost of the building supplies necessary to construct the homes on the land owned by Alger.

By investing in the land, Alger was investing in the future of the community by dramatically lowering the cost of home ownership and making it possible for families who never would have qualified for a loan to own their own home. In most cases, the $50,000 mortgage resulted in lowering their housing expenses from $1,000 a month to about $350. In the future, when they had built equity in the home and had increased their income, they could purchase the land as well.

About half of the families who applied for loans were approved. These fifty families then participated in group counseling sessions that had two specific goals. The first was to learn more about each family's ability to contribute and work toward building a supportive community. The second purpose of the sessions was to teach conflict resolution skills and to provide some basic guidance in how to deal with issues like violence and drugs.

The counselors then prepared individual assessments of each of the finalists in the form of family biographies. These reports were submitted to a panel that selected the six families that would participate in the first phase of the program. Then the real work began. Families were now required to build their own homes.

Every weekend for months, the husbands and wives would show up at the job site and work with the other couples, actually cutting the studs, pounding the nails, and hauling the plywood up onto the roof. It was hard, backbreaking work, particularly for those who had never picked up a hammer before, but it was the most important step in the process. You can't create a community out of whole cloth. Things like loyalty and commitment to a place come from shared experience, a sense that a group of people have invested equally in the creation of the little piece of the world you share together. As the families built the six homes together, no one knew which house was the one they would soon own, so they went about the work as if every house was theirs. They learned to work together, resolving their differences just as they were learning the practical skills necessary to care for and maintain a home.

Today that first small section of the subdivision that will one day be a neighborhood of seventy families now has eight new homes with fresh paint and plush green lawns. There are toddlers playing in the cul de sac and the sound of their voices mixes with the noise coming from the hammering going on nearby. Patti Lyons has just arrived after another eighteen-hour flight from the Philippines. She is standing on the plywood deck of a single-family home under construction in the second phase of the development where six new families are working. Standing with her is Caroline Oda, who oversees the foundation's work in Hawaii.

Caroline says, "Consuelo's vision is something that motivates us all, not only the staff, but the people all around us whose lives have been changed by what she has given."

Patti nods her agreement and together they turn and look behind them at the five other houses rising out of the old pasture. Then Patti speaks. "We call this neighborhood Ke Aka Hoona, which means 'Spirit of Consuelo.' The streets are named with Hawaiian words that stand for the values she left with us. They mean peace, nurturance, security, and helping hands." Patty turns for a moment and looks over the new phase of the project, and you can see that she is thinking about the future. She raises her hand and points to a line of saplings that have been planted along the side of the new roads. "See those trees?" she says. "Those are shower trees. They were Consuelo's favorite. As this community grows, those trees will grow and bloom as well, and someday, far in the future, they will shower colorful petals down on the children who play below them, and the spirit of Consuelo will live on forever."

The Magic

*These simple acts of kindness
are the footsteps on the road of
happiness. They are what carry us
down the dusty roads of Galilee.*

W HEN WE STARTED the two-year quest to discover
the magic that occurs when one human being
helps another, we asked not to be judged by the
answers we provided, but by the questions we asked.

So we went to the places where visionaries dwell with
our cameras shouldered and our notebooks at the ready —
inquisitors in the land of lost causes, some would scoff.

We thought otherwise, but our motives were not pure. We
wanted to do something different and unique in the world of
television, because it would make us feel good. Who knows,
we might even earn some money and advance our careers
in the process. It wasn't the furthest thing from our minds.
Spending two years traveling to some of the most exotic places
in the world didn't seem too tough to take either.

We were wrong. Once we made the conscious decision to
try to *feel* our way through the stories, much of it was too
tough to take. You see, journalists are supposed to be objective. In our culture, that is translated into meaning that they
are required to record the hard, cold facts and leave the in-
terpretation to the viewers at home. In our case, however,
we weren't interested in the facts. We wanted to record the
feelings and leave it up to the viewers to go out and find
the facts.

The toughest thing to take was living through Judy Mayotte's nightmare with her and trying to make sense out of the
tragedy. It was the second show we produced. We had already

had a glimpse of what level of emotion we must be prepared to endure after watching Laura and Dan Grasso hand their son, Vinny, over to the transplant surgeons. But in Africa, on that field of bleached bones, we discovered that this thing was bigger and more important than any of us had ever imagined. We learned that it wasn't about us anymore. It was about them.

Our third program was the Human Service Alliance. It came at just the right time, finding us with our hearts laid bare. When we first arrived in Winston-Salem, the program struck us as being a little odd. Everything seemed too good to be true, and we kept waiting for some weird cultish angle to rear its ugly head. Our healthy skepticism melted away when we learned that there was no charismatic leader and no common commitment to a particular religious philosophy.

Once we began to relax, sit back, and allow ourselves to absorb the concepts that this extraordinary group of people had discovered, we began to understand the magnitude of what we were witnessing. Toward the end of the shoot, we began to feel like a group of explorers who announced one day that they were going to travel to the ends of the earth in search of the holy grail of human emotion, only to discover the great prize on the baggage turnstile during a layover in Winston-Salem.

Nonetheless, the HSA program became the rudder that helped to guide us through the rest of the series. No matter where we went, we saw the shadows of what we had learned at HSA cast across every story we encountered.

The idea that service is about *being*, rather than *doing*, blossomed in an episode that profiled the Maryknoll Sisters, an order of Catholic nuns who work with the poor all over the world.

In El Salvador, the land of martyrs, we lived with a group of Maryknoll Sisters who taught us how deeply the commitment can be felt and to what extraordinary lengths a person will go to simply be with the people. The Maryknollers believe in a concept called accompaniment. What they mean by this is that they are called to be with the poorest of the poor, no matter where that road may take them.

We visited the grave site of two of their Sisters who were

Sister Mary Annel brings her medical training to a new AIDS prevention program in El Salvador, a country on the brink of a major epidemic.

Cité Soleil, Haiti

raped and murdered in El Salvador in December of 1980, along with two other church women, because they chose to accompany the poor who were being oppressed, tortured, and murdered by a sadistic government.

Today, Sister Mary Annel, a practicing physician, is walking the same streets in San Salvador that Sisters Maura Clarke and Ita Ford traveled before their murders. Today the Maryknollers in El Salvador are accompanying the people on the latest crisis in their lives: AIDS. More than seventy thousand Salvadorans are infected with the virus, a relatively small number, but world health organizations predict that unless preventative actions are taken immediately that number will explode over the next five years.

Sister Mary Annel along with Sisters Lorraine Beinkafner and Bernadette Lynch are initiating education and training programs that are directed at increasing the awareness of how to prevent the disease. All the while they work in hospitals and clinics sharing time with people who are already infected and helping them through the last days.

Sister Mary Annel took us to the home of Archbishop Romero, and we stood in his simple bedroom as she told us how in 1980 he called upon government soldiers to defy the orders of their commanders and stop the acts of violence against innocent people. Then we walked together to the church where, a week after his sermon to the soldiers, he was gunned down while standing at the altar celebrating Mass.

Sister Mary Annel taught us that *being* is so much more difficult than *doing*. She was working in Guatemala in 1980 at the time of the Sisters' death.

She had been in Guatemala organizing and training health care providers to work in the vast number of villages that had no medical services. She was at the hospital one day when a squad of government soldiers from a nearby army base came in with a badly injured rebel soldier. The young man had been cornered at the edge of a cliff by government troops. He chose to dive, head first, onto the rocks below rather than risk betraying his comrades during the torture that would follow his capture. Remarkably, he survived the fall and the troops carried him into the hospital. They ordered Sister Mary Annel to wake up their unconscious prisoner so they could begin questioning him.

It was the latest event in an escalating campaign of terror that placed Sister Mary Annel at a critical juncture where outrage and moral indignation ran headlong into a lifelong commitment to peace. Just a few weeks earlier, several of her close friends had been forced to participate in citizen patrols that were required to search for guerillas on the outskirts of their village.

One night her friends stumbled across a small group of young rebels hiding in the bush. Fearing that they and their families would be killed by government soldiers if they did not act, they turned them over to government soldiers. The prisoners were brutally tortured during a long interrogation. But the nightmare had just begun. After the soldiers had extracted all the information they could from their captives, they brought them back to the village where they had been caught. The soldiers ordered all the townspeople out of their homes and assembled them in the village square. There they forced the citizen patrol members who had captured the guerillas to form a circle around the bloody prisoners kneeling in the street. Each patrol member was handed a club. Then the soldiers raised their machine guns and ordered the citizen patrol to beat the prisoners to death in front of the town. They did as they were told.

Day after day, week after week, the brutality grew worse, and as it did, Sister Mary Annel wondered where she would draw the line. At what point should she stop *being* and start *doing* something in defense of her people. She decided that the line had to be drawn at the point when one of her patients was threatened.

That threat came the day the comatose rebel arrived at the hospital. Sister Mary Annel tried everything to convince the soldiers that they would never be able to question the young man. She hooked him up to every tube and wire she could find to accentuate the gravity of his injury. Then she went back again to her office hoping the soldiers would go away. Instead, they ripped the intravenous tubes from his body, deposited him on a stretcher, and prepared to take him back to the army base where they would use their own methods to make him talk. Sister Mary Annel saw his stretcher pass by her doorway. She leapt to her feet and raced for the door. Just before she burst out into the hallway, other members of the medical staff grabbed her and dragged her back into the room. Wrestling with her, they pleaded with her not to intercede. If she did, the entire hospital staff and all of the patients would be labeled guerilla sympathizers. They could all be killed. Sister Mary Annel discovered how much harder *being* was than *doing*.

After we left the Human Service Alliance, we began to view the world of philanthropy as the coliseum where our best intentions are thrown to a pair of lions named money and ego. Life had led us to believe that they might be invincible, so we surmised that discovering the magic had something to do with holding them at bay. If you could only find a way, as the people at HSA seemed to have done, to tame the ferocious beast, then you might find the passageway to utopia.

Then two new stories came along and taught us that nothing in life is so simple. Christian Relief Services demonstrated that money doesn't have to be a carnivore of our kind hearts. Money can be a beast of burden that transports our intentions for good or for evil, wherever we want it to go. What CRS has done is go out across America and herd these good intentions together and dutifully shepherd them to where they are needed most.

The Alger Foundation demonstrated the awesome power our desire to serve can have to transcend any imaginable obstacle, even traversing the boundary between life and death, riding through time atop the almighty dollar.

As we traveled around the world interacting with people who seemed to live life by a different code of conduct, we were constantly pulled back by gnawing doubts about what we were discovering. The biggest of the questions posed by our ever-skeptical left brains was why wasn't everyone doing what these people were doing? The answer ultimately seemed to be that we are all, in one way or another, traveling on the same road to the same destination, but the journey is filled with detours, many of which lead down blind alleys. No matter how hard our analytical minds try to con us into believing that pursuits such as occupational success, athletic accomplishment and even artistic fulfillment are highways to happiness, it often doesn't work out that way.

Out of all of this emerges the realization that there might be an elusive set of navigational laws that once learned could be shared with others to help them find their way. We mused earlier about the possibility that human emotion might operate by a set of laws that are different from those that govern the physical universe. Suppose for a minute there are two worlds. One is the physical universe where all of science operates by a concrete set of quantum laws. Then there is another place where human feelings dwell. There is another set of laws that govern this place.

We need to learn the ways of the other world because they are the stepping stones that might lead to truth. But there are two kinds of truth. There is universal truth and there is personal truth. In the two years we spent traveling around the world poking questions at what we perceived to be the great new issue of our time, we did arrive at some personal truths. Using the words "I" and "me" seem out of place in a book about "them," but talking about "our" personal truth is a conflict in terms.

I can only speak for me, but there are some profound lessons I have learned in the world where visionaries dwell. First, for me at least, there truly seems to be a direct correlation between the degree of service one experiences and the level of happiness one feels. The physical act of giving appears to stimulate a specific and predictable emotional outcome. This emotion is as real and at least as relevant to the human condition as intellectual thought. In fact, objective intellectual analysis seems to lead to the conclusion that we think what we think because of what we feel.

Deepak Chopra, M.D., eloquently pointed out in books like *Quantum Healing* and *Ageless Body, Timeless Mind* that when a person feels beauty, love, harmony, tranquility, admiration, wonder, or amazement, very real things occur in the physical world. Specific chemicals are manufactured in the brain when we feel happy, are suddenly startled, or experience frustrations. They flow through the body, setting off a dizzying array of predictable biological events that literally alter the chemical composition of who we are.

Once you accept the scientific reality that human emotion causes specific and predictable chemical events that can be analyzed and proven on a quantum mechanical level, you're confronted with several huge questions. What does the emotion come from? Why do we feel the things we do? What role does the creation of these feelings play in determining who we are? What came first, the feeling or the feeler?

All of this is pretty heady stuff well outside the purview of a bunch of documentarians, but as we said at the outset, our role is not to provide the answers but to inspire people to start asking the questions.

If the visionaries have their way, a hundred generations from now our descendants will look back at all we have created and marvel at what a long, circuitous route we traveled to arrive back at where it all began: one human being loving another human being.

On the other hand, the long road around might be the only way to get back to where we started in the first place. As was the case for the early explorers looking for a new world, maybe the only way to reach the east is to sail west.

When you look closely at this thing we have called the "magic," you discover a structure and set of rules that seem to be a microcosmic chart for this seemingly endless journey humanity has been traveling to get back to where we began. Such lofty concepts are better left to greater minds and more experienced explorers in the domain of the human psyche, but having spent some time on the road toward emotional well-being, we can at least report on the traveling conditions.

All the rules of the road share one common trait. Like the human brain that produces separate, contradictory points of view from its competing hemispheres, the compass settings leading to emotional well-being seem always to point in opposite directions. Therefore when you're traveling through life, the first test to determine the validity of a particular course toward happiness ought to be whether or not it's paradoxical.

Every visionary we met, in different ways and with different words, attested to this fundamental truth. In Haiti, Gladys Sylvestre acquired the resources she needed to accomplish incredible feats by consciously giving up the need for the resources and committing herself to the daily act of giving. In Colombia, Father Xavier took thousands of the children considered so worthless they are named "the disposables" and transformed them into some of the country's most valuable citizens. How did he do it? By instituting a formula that was fundamentally paradoxical. He created value by giving them a commodity that cost nothing. He gave them love and affection and they produced the rest.

On the Pine Ridge Indian Reservation in South Dakota, two centuries of failed and misguided attempts to serve Native Americans are being corrected by removing the old, non-paradoxical approach and implementing a synergistic program that requires everyone to take the long way around to get back to the beginning. Everything that has ever been done on the Indian reservations in America failed because the government saw a problem and administered a direct solution. The "people-are-hungry-give-them-food" kind of answer in the end deprived the people of dignity and the ability to help themselves. The paradoxical approach requires that you supply food by providing something inedible, like seeds, plows and wells. Only then can the people walk their own walk and arrive at a place of dignity.

Nowhere is this truth more evident than at the Human Service Alliance, where they discovered the magic by connecting with people during the ultimate moment of human disconnection: death. Through this process, they started down the road that led to other great contradictions. They discovered that self-worth was achieved by removing the self from the equation. They found materialistic good fortune the moment they stopped trying to earn money. In the process, they made an extraordinary discovery: life wasn't about them, it was about us — all of us. Individual fulfillment and ultimate happiness comes not from seeking it but by giving it to others.

When you begin to view life's journey from this perspective, a new reality emerges. Judy Mayotte gave us a hint at how to see this new view. A few days before the tragedy that would take her leg, she said it was all about "how we walk through life, how we walk down the dusty roads of Galilee."

It's the same message we have been receiving from all the visionaries in different ways. You can call it living in the moment, involving yourself in the details and releasing yourself from the outcome, stepping into the unknown, an act of faith. It's all the same. They are all saying that happiness is in the walking, not in the arriving. After all, no matter what we do during our lifetime, we all end up at the same place. When we reach the end of the road, we discover we are all back where we began.

So what is the moral of the story? What is the single most important lesson learned on the two-hundred-thousand-mile quest to discover the magic that occurs when one human being helps another. It is this.

It all comes back to the power of personal perspective. Every event that occurs in our life is a signpost pointing in opposite directions. Some of these milestones mark the places where enormous tragedies occurred; but no matter how deep the pain, we still must choose which way to go. The magic is in the choice. At every juncture, we are given the power to alter dramatically our view of the world in which we live. Time and time again we saw people who lived through some of the most devastating experiences imaginable. Some found happiness and others did not. Why?

The signpost has two words on it. One points to the left and says "fear." The other directs you to the right and says "love."

If you choose to do nothing the current of life will carry you to the left. If you take one positive step forward, your foot will land on the right road.

The magic that occurs when one human being helps another is that these simple acts of kindness are the footsteps on the road of happiness. They are what carry us down the dusty roads of Galilee.

I wonder why that is?